THE
ILLUSTRATED
HERBAL
HANDBOOK

by

ADELMA GRENIER SIMMONS

HAWTHORN BOOKS, INC.
Publishers
New York

The herbs listed in this volume appear alphabetically under their horticultural names. For the reader's convenience an index of common names of herbs, when these differ from their horticultural names, appears on page 124.

The Wide World of the Herbalist

Through the centuries in which man has explored and recorded his findings in the world of herbs, funds of information have widened and accumulated. Herb lore was collected by men and women in all walks of life— medicine men and sincere scholars can be contrasted with charlatans who, snatched at every herbal straw to further their own fortunes.

Great poets like Vergil wrote about herbs, and peasants made memorable verses about them or told and retold tales that have become our folklore. Kings experimented with herbal medicines, and even the august Charlemagne gave orders for the planting of herbs and vegetables. His is probably the much-quoted definition of herbs: "The friend of the physician and the pride of cooks."

All of us who study, write, talk about, or grow herbs owe a debt to the past, for herbal history invests even our most unprepossessing plants with an aura of romantic legend.

We do not stand alone in the wide world of herbs, for there are many great gardeners there to keep us company—men like Francis Bacon, essayist, planner and planter of gardens for gentlemen.

The history of herbs starts five thousand years before the Christian era. The ancient Chaldeans, Chinese, Egyptians, and Assyrians had schools of herbalists. Their learning came in precious scrolls and by word of mouth through teachers, necromancers, and astrologers to the Greeks, who through their philosophers and historians, particularly Aristotle and Plato, and their physicians Theophrastus and Hippocrates advanced the use of herbs.

It was in the first century that Dioscorides became famous in botany and medicine. A Greek from Asia Minor, he traveled with the Roman legions, probably as an army doctor. He studied the healing herbs of the world he knew and recorded his findings in *Materia*

Medica, which dealt with more than five hundred plants. His original work was destroyed, but a Byzantine copy dated about A.D. 512 survived the years and has been studied in facsimile by many generations.

Pliny the Elder, a contemporary of Dioscorides, wrote of many things in his *Natural History*—both the practical and the fabulous. Through his pages roam birds, animals, and plants that never were.

After Pliny the succeeding centuries brought us the period of monastery herbals. The cultivation of plants in the quiet world of the cloister produced many treatises on growing herbs and vegetables.

It is in the sixteenth and seventeenth centuries that we come to the English herbals that are best known and most frequently quoted. Here the names of Bancke (1525), *The Grete Herball* (1526), and Turner (1568) lead us to the most quoted herbal of all, John Gerard's *The Herball or Generall Historie of Plantes,* published in 1597. Gerard was a barber-surgeon whose greatest interest was gardening. Fashionable Holborn in England was the place where he cultivated the long list of plants that furnished subject matter for his pen and a garden for the study, wonder, and admiration of his contemporaries. Although the years and the advance of science may have taken some luster from Gerard's name, he is still read for many truths that bear repeating.

John Parkinson was herbalist to Charles I and is remembered for a book published in 1629 called *Paradisi in Sole Paradisus Terrestris.* Later he produced a much larger work called *Theatrum Botanicum: The Theatre of Plants, or an Herball of a Large Extent.*

Astrology and the herbalist have ever seemed to go together, but in the seventeenth century the vogue of tying each herb to a star was at its height, and Nicholas Culpeper (1616–1654) made the most of the fad. He established a practice as astrologer and physician at Spitalfields and caused great indignation among medical men of his day by publishing *A Physicall Directory,* an unauthorized translation of the *Pharmacopoeia* issued by the College of Physicians.

THE
ILLUSTRATED
HERBAL
HANDBOOK

K.B.

ACHILLEA

Compositae

Thou pretty herb of Venus tree
Thy true name it is Yarrow
Now who my bosom friend must be,
Pray tell thou me to-morrow.
                    —J. O. Halliwell

Common yarrow (*Achillea millefolium*), according to legend, was used by Achilles to stop bleeding wounds of his soldiers, hence the name "military herb." Yarrow tea was once used in treating fevers, colds, and kidney disorders. The leaves were used fresh in salads and dried for snuff.

Description:
Hardy perennial, to 2 ft. Leaves gray-green, finely divided, giving name "milfoil" (thousand-leaved). Flowers grayish white or pale lavender in flattened cymes. *A. m. rosea* (red yarrow) has dark red or bright pink flowers. *A. filipendulina*, 4 to 5 ft., has large dark yellow flowers; its varieties range from pale cream to the golden yellow of 'Gold Plate.' *A. ptarmica* ('The Pearl' or sneezewort), 2 ft., has white flowers. The dwarf yarrows (*A. nana, A. tomentosa*, and *A. t. webbiana*) make good ground covers.

Uses:
Flower arrangements, fresh or dried. Ironclad garden perennials for late spring and summer color.

Culture:
Full sun and well-drained soil. Propagate by dividing roots, spring or fall; or transplant self-sown seedlings.

3

K.B.

ACONITUM

Ranunculaceae

Our land is from the rage of tigers freed,
Nor nourishes the lion's angry seed,
Nor pois'nous aconite is here produced,
Or grows unknown, or is, when known refused.
          —John Dryden

The root of aconite (*Aconitum napellus*) has long been known as a source of poison once used on arrows to destroy wolves, hence the name "wolfbane." In the middle ages, this plant was known as monkshood, or helmet flower owing to the shape of the flower.

℞ *Description:*
Hardy perennial, to 4 ft. Leaves divided two or three times into narrow segments. Flowers in blue spikes. Old roots last only a year and new plants are produced by young shoots from the parent. The 'Sparks' variety is considered best for late summer color in the garden. It sends spikes of dark blue to a height of 5 ft. *A. n. bicolor* has blue and white flowers. *A. fischeri*, 2 to 3 ft., has dark blue blooms. *A. f. wilsoni*, 6 to 7 ft., has mauve flowers.

℞ *Uses:*
Outstanding for late summer and fall color, but dangerous to have around children. Medicinally it is to be used only by a physician.

℞ *Culture:*
Partial shade with evenly moist, rich soil. Propagate by division of the roots in autumn. Spring-sown seeds reach maturity in two or three years.

5

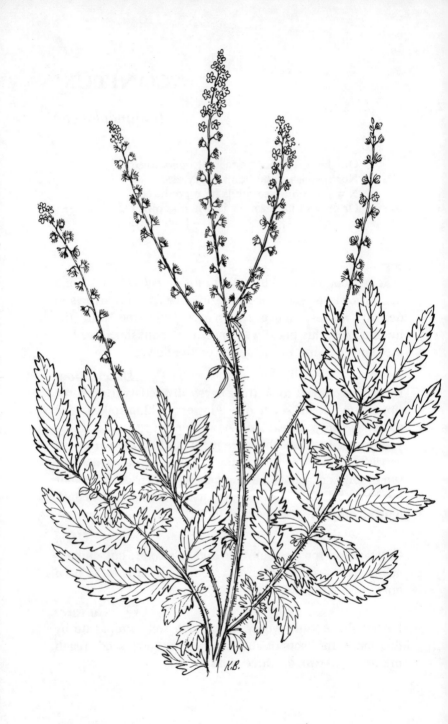

AGRIMONIA

Rosaceae

If it be leyd under mann's heed,
He shal sleepyn as he were deed;
He shal never drede ne wakyn
Till fro under his heed it be takyn.
                    —Old English Medical Manuscript

Common agrimony (*Agrimonia eupatoria*), also known as church steeples and cocklebur, received its generic name from the Greek word *argemone*, applied to plants that were healing to the eyes. The specific name *eupatoria* refers to Mithridates Eupator, a famous king who concocted remedies. Agrimony was once used for jaundice and skin disorders, and with mugwort and vinegar as a back rub. It is still collected as a medicinal herb in England.

Description:
Hardy perennial, 1 to 3 ft. Leaves similar to those of a wild rose. Flowers yellow, small, and numerous, occurring close together on a slender spike from June to September. The plant is downy and gives off a pleasant odor. It grows wild in Scotland.

Uses:
The whole plant, dried, is ground to be made into a tea said to be excellent as a spring tonic. Historically, the yellow blossoms have served as a source of dye.

Culture:
Dry soil with full sun or light shade. Propagate by sowing seeds collected from a dried spike. Germinates easily and, once established, it self-sows.

7

K.B.

AJUGA

Labiatae

With hearts responsive
And enfranchised eyes,
We thank thee Lord,
For those first tiny, prayerful folded hands
That pierce the winter's crust ...
— John Oxenham

Bugleweed, blue bugle, or carpenter's herb (*Ajuga reptans*) was once a medicinal plant used for hemorrhage, and it is reputed to have a mild narcotic action similar to that of digitalis.

Description:
Hardy perennial, to 5 ins., astringent, bitter, and aromatic. Leaves occur in rosettes that form a ground cover. Flowers clear blue on short spikes in early spring. *A. r. alba* has white flowers and green foliage. *A. r. variegata* has blue flowers and green leaves variegated with creamy white.

Uses:
Invaluable as a ground cover. It will thrive where few other herbs will grow and may be used where grass is difficult to establish, as under trees and shrubs.

Culture:
Needs shade and well-drained soil. Multiplies rapidly by means of underground stolons. Solid beds of ajuga need to be thinned every year. Divide and transplant in spring or fall.

9

ALLIUM

Liliaceae

Let onion atoms lurk within the bowl
And, half suspected, animate the whole.
—Sydney Smith

The shallot (*Allium cepa ascalonicum*) is considered the most delectable of all onions. At one time it was known as eschalot, brought back by the Crusaders from Ascalon, an ancient city in West Palestine, and introduced into England and the Continent by them.

☙ *Description:*

Perennial bulb, 6 ins., onion-like. Blooms rarely.

☙ *Uses:*

Cloves of the bulbs are used in sauces for meats, with steaks, in dressings, in vinegars, for salads, and in sauce for fish. Harvest when the bulblets have multiplied so that the thickened clump forms a mound that rises partially out of the ground, usually between the first and the middle of September. Dig, tie in bunches, and hang to cure in an airy place. When dry, store in a ventilated sack, preferably a real onion bag, removing one clove from each clump for next year's seed. Hang in a cool, but frost-free, dry place. If left in the ground over winter the bulbs frequently rot.

☙ *Culture:*

Full sun in well-drained, fertile soil. Plant the sets in early spring, covering to a depth of twice their length.

11

K.B.

ALLIUM

Liliaceae

This is every cook's opinion,
No savory dish without an onion,
But lest your kissing should be spoiled
Your onions must be fully boiled.
  —Jonathan Swift

Top onion (*Allium cepa viviparum*) also known as perennial or Egyptian onion, is a practical onion to grow for use in early spring. It can also be a really handsome back border for the culinary garden. This plant was symbolic, to the Egyptians, of the Universe. Vast quantities of it were consumed by the workmen who built the pyramids, for Herodotus said it took nine tons of gold to pay for the "pungent onion."

Description:
Hardy perennial, 3 ft., with succulent hollow stems, ballooned toward the top, and crowned by a head of new plants. The weight of these increases until the whole stem falls to the ground, and there the bulbs take root and form another colony.

Uses:
Cut the spears of the young leaves as they appear in the spring for salads and to use with sorrel soup. Use the bulblets like small onions (they are very strong), or pickle as cocktail onions. Cut plants back after they have borne the top bulblets, and fresh green shoots will grow again.

Culture:
Full sun in well-cultivated, fertile garden soil.

13

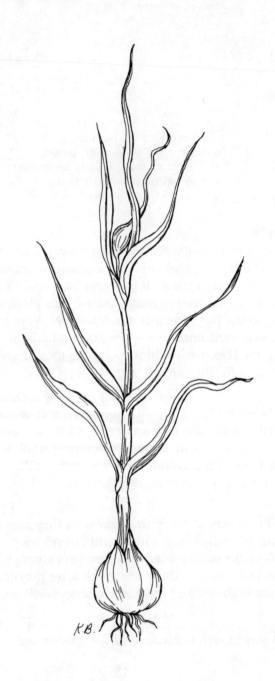

ALLIUM

Liliaceae

And, most dear actors, eat no onions nor garlic,
for we are to utter sweet breath.
　　　　　　　　　　　—Shakespeare

Garlic (*Allium sativum*) has been important from
ancient times, and is still a part of the Hebrew Talmudic
rule which decrees that it be used in certain dishes. There
is a legend that garlic came into the world on Satan's left
foot, while onion came on his right. In the past, it was
fed to fighting cocks and animals and to athletes to give
them strength. Ramson or wild garlic received its name
from ram, alluding to the strong smell.

　　　　　　　　　　　　　　　　Description:
Hardy perennial, 2 ft. I find that the giant garlic or rocam-
bole (*A. scorodoprasum*) is much more interesting to
grow. It is similar in appearance to the Egyptian onion,
producing new plants at the top of very slender stems, to
3 ft. The bulbs are about ⅛ in. across, tightly interlaced,
smelling strongly of garlic and useful in cheese mixtures
or as a substitute for garlic.

　　　　　　　　　　　　　　　　　Uses:
Harvest the bulbs of garlic after the tops die down and
store for the winter in open mesh bags. This is such a
common seasoning that its uses do not need to be out-
lined. In fact, I do not consider this a worthwhile garden
plant, as it is so easily obtainable from the warm, sunny
climates of Texas, California, and Louisiana where it is
grown commercially.

15

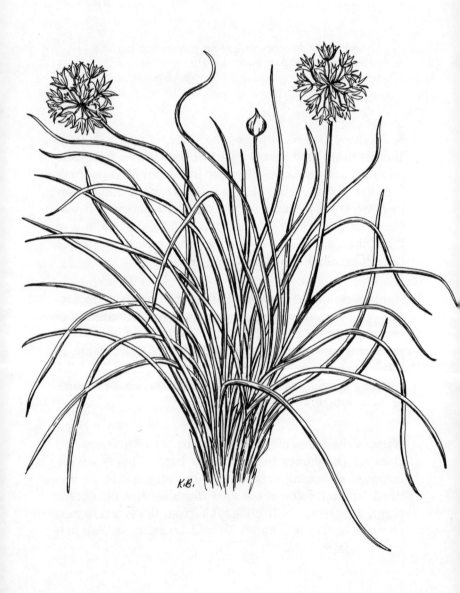

K.B.

ALLIUM

Liliaceae

They are indeed a kind of leeks, hot and dry in the fourth degree, and so under the domination of Mars . . . if they be eaten raw they send up very hurtful vapours to the brain causing troublesome sleep and spoiling the eyesight.
—Nicholas Culpeper

Chives (*Allium schoenoprasum*) is one of the most familiar of all plants to the herb grower. The plants are cultivated for the onion-flavored, edible leaves, as a border for the culinary garden, and for the heads of lilac-colored flowers which may be used in arrangements.

Description:
Hardy perennial to 1 ft., producing fountains of hollow, cylindrical leaves. The variety 'Ruby Gem' has gray foliage and pink-ruby flowers; another variety, *A. tuberosum*, often called garlic chives or Chinese chives, blooms naturally in July and August, but is forced by florists for early spring flower shows. It has wider leaves than common chives, and the white flowers grow in attractive starlike clusters on long slender stems, very fragrant.

Uses:
Cut the leaves for soups and salads from early spring on; use in cream cheese mixtures, with mashed potatoes, in hamburger, or with eggs in omelettes. Chives can be frozen fresh, or dried for winter seasoning.

Culture:
Sunny, well-drained garden loam. Sow seeds in spring or fall. Divide established clumps every third or fourth year.

17

K.B.

ANETHUM

Umbelliferae

Therewith her Vervain and her Dill
That hindereth witches of their will.
—Michael Drayton

Dill (*Anethum graveolens*) received its name from the old Norse word *dilla*, to lull, referring to the soothing properties of the plant. It has been used by magicians to cast spells and employed as a charm against such spells.

Description:

Hardy annual sometimes classed as a biennial, 2 to 2½ ft., native of Mediterranean shores and southern Russia. It grows in the grain fields of Spain, Portugal, and Italy. The plant is upright, branching out from a single stalk with the feathery leaves, known as "dill weed." Flowers in flat terminal umbels, numerous and yellow, followed by "dill seed" in midsummer. The seeds are pungent tasting and retain their potency for three years or more.

Uses:

Harvest dill weed (the leaves) early in summer, then chop fine and dry in a basket, turning often. Sprinkle on fish, salad, and soups during winter. Harvest the seeds as soon as the head is ripe, otherwise they will drop off and be lost. Large umbels of green dill are used to flavor cucumber pickles.

Culture:

Rich, sandy, well-drained soil in full sun. Propagate by sowing seeds in the spring. If all seed heads are not harvested, dill may self-sow.

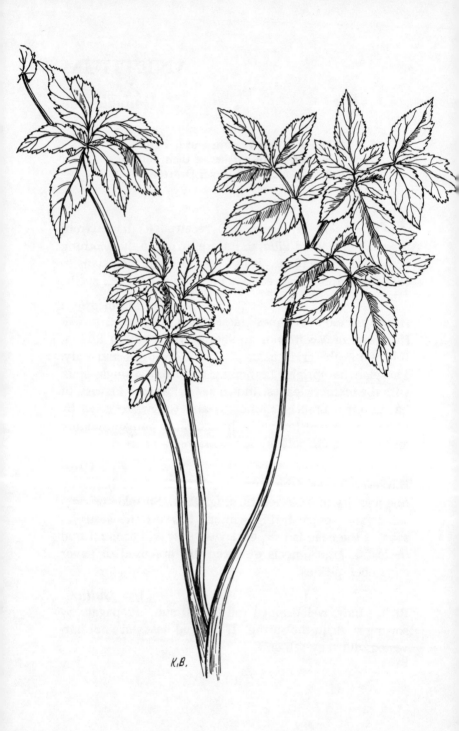

K.B.

ANGELICA

Umbelliferae

Contagious aire ingendring pestilence,
Infects not those who in their mouth have Tae'en
Angelica, that happy Counterbane.
Sent down from heaven by some Celestial scout
As well the name and nature both avow't.
—DuBartas

Angelica (*Angelica archangelica*) was once used in pagan ceremonies in Iceland. Later it was adapted by Christians for use at the springtime festival of the Annunciation. The plant blooms in some parts of the world on May 8, the Day of St. Michael the Archangel, and hence it was considered a charm against evil spirits. Medicinally, it was used against contagion and for purifying the blood.

Description:
Hardy biennial, grown as a perennial if the flower stalks are not allowed to develop and set seed. If allowed to bloom and seed, the old plant dies, but its place is taken in the spring by self-sown seedlings. Grows 4 to 7 ft. tall. Leaves celery-like, divided into three-part leaflets, strongly aromatic of gin and juniper. Flowers greenish white in spectacular umbels.

Uses:
Seeds in making a liqueur, in vermouth and chartreuse, and as a flavoring for wines; also in perfumes. The candied stems are a traditional French decoration for Christmas cakes and buns; also made into jams and jellies.

Culture:
Rich, moist soil and partial shade in a cool part of the garden. Propagate by sowing seeds immediately after they ripen on the plant, that is, in the fall.

21

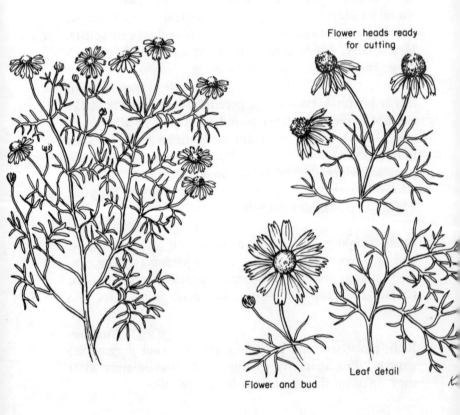

Flower heads ready
for cutting

Flower and bud

Leaf detail

ANTHEMIS

Compositae

For though the camomile, the more it is trodden
on, the faster it grows, yet youth, the more
it is wasted, the sooner it wears.
                                          —Shakespeare

Englishcamomile (*Anthemis nobilis*) also known as
ground apple, was once considered the plants' physician,
as some gardeners believed that planting this herb among
drooping and sickly plants would revive them. The
Spanish call it *manzanilla*, and use it to flavor one of their
lightest and driest sherries. Most of camomile's history
relates to its use as a tea in relieving nervousness, for
neuralgia, pains in the head, and nervous colic. It is also
the tea given to Peter Rabbit after his famous bout with
Mr. McGregor. Early herbals recommend it for sleepless-
ness and as a sure cure for nightmares. Camomile lawns
were once possible in the moist climate of England, but
our climate is too rugged to grow them in this capacity.

Description:
A creeping perennial, about 1 in. high, except to 12 ins.
while in bloom. Foliage very fine and fernlike. The flowers are white daisies with yellow centers.

Uses:
The dried flower heads are brewed for the tea.

Culture:
Sun to partial shade in moist, well-drained soil. Sow seeds
in spring or fall, or purchase plants. Once established,
camomiles will self-sow.

23

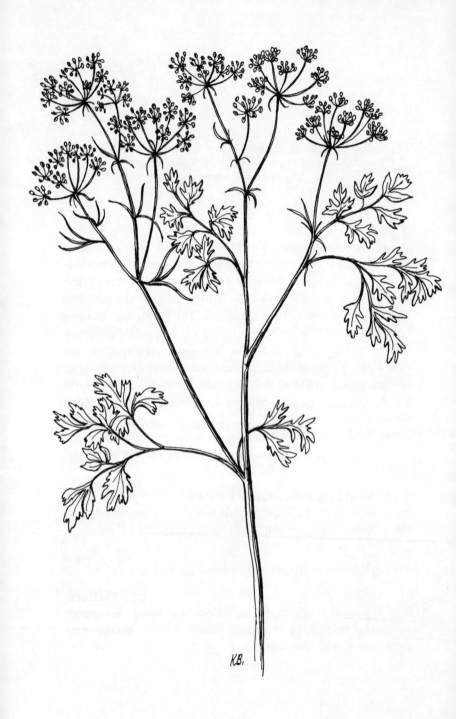

KB.

ANTHRISCUS

Umbelliferae

Sweete Spanish Chervile, ought never to be wanting in our sallets—for it is exceeding wholesome and charming to the spirits. . . . this . . . is used in tarts and serves alone for divers sauces.

—John Evelyn

Chervil (*Anthriscus cerefolium*), also called beaked parsley and French parsley, is the gourmet's parsley. True chervil is often confused with sweet cicely which is sometimes called "sweet chervil." Therefore, when early writers speak of chervil, they mean sweet cicely or sweet chervil (*Myrrhis odorata*), not the plant discussed here.

❦ *Description:*
Annual, 1 to 2 ft. Leaves alternate, fernlike, and spreading. The plant resembles Italian parsley, though more delicate, and turns reddish in the fall. Small white flowers in compound umbels.

❦ *Uses:*
Attractive in garden. Use leaves in salads and soups, with oysters, and as a garnish. The curled variety is best to grow as it has the flavor of anise.

❦ *Culture:*
Moist, well-drained soil in partial shade. Sow seeds early in spring for an early summer crop; sow again in late summer for a fall harvest and one in early spring. Self-sows year after year.

25

VARIED ARTEMISIAS: (top left) tarragon *Artemisia Dracunculus sativa*, (top right) southernwood *A. Abrotanum*, (center) mugwort *A. vulgaris*, (bottom left) 'Silver King' *A. ludoviciana albula*, (bottom right) wormwood *A. Absinthium*

ARTEMISIA

Compositae

What savour is best, if physic be true,
For places infected than wormwood and rue?
—Thomas Tusser

Artemisias are divided into decorative types, mugworts, southernwoods, and wormwoods. Tarragon alone is primarily a seasoning herb.

The Decorative Artemisias

A. ludoviciana grows to 6 ft. The foliage is nearly white. *A. l. albula,* the popular 'Silver King,' is valued for its cloud effect in the garden and for dried winter decorations. *A. Purshiana,* sometimes known as cudweed wormwood, has a broader leaf than 'Silver King.' It grows to 2 ft. and makes an excellent gray note in the border. 'Silver Mound' artemisia, *A. Schmidtiana nana,* is elegant and extravagant. The plant is hardy and easily divided. *A. tridentata,* the sagebrush of the West, grows to 12 ft. and has highly scented leaves.

After *albula* is cut in early autumn, it may be dried into decorative material.

A. ludoviciana is propagated by root division in spring or fall. 'Silver King' seed panicles turn brown or black if the plant is allowed to stand, but the garden will be bare of it if it is cut back. Grow two rows; cut back one in late summer, and allow the other seeds to ripen. Divide two-year-old clumps of 'Silver Mound' during September, giving them time to get set before cold weather. They thrive in dry, sunny places. They succumb to winter only in heavy, rich soil that holds too much water.

The Mugworts

A. annua, the sweet mugwort, grows in one season to the
height of a small tree; it is green, very fragrant, and
excellent for dried arrangements. *A. lactiflora,* also
called sweet mugwort, has fragrant white blossoms with
leaves greener than they are gray on a plant 5 ft. tall.
A. vulgaris, the common mugwort or German *Beifuss,*
grows to 4 or 5 ft., has silver-backed and cut leaves, and
is decorative if controlled.

Dry mugwort for arrangements and for use in goose
stuffings.

Cut many roots and remove seedlings each year to
control plants.

The Southernwoods

All plants in this classification come under the name
A. Abrotanum, and they are known by scents of lemon,
camphor, and tangerine. *A. A. camphorata* and *A. A.
limoneum* are difficult to tell apart in certain seasons.
The lemon-scented one is grayer than the camphor type,
is more upright in growth, and is harder to propagate by
root division. It flowers less often and takes longer
to show green in spring. The camphor artemisia is
likely to sprawl along the ground if not frequently transplanted. When properly cared for it makes an attractive
hedge, 2 to 3 ft. high. It is winter hardy and emits an
odor like camphor. Tangerine-scented southernwood is
a tall, willow herb, growing to 7 or 8 ft., that combines
well with the lower-growing artemisias. It is notably late
to leaf out in spring. Two other species, *A. borealis* and
A. glacialis (or *A. laxa*), are sometimes grouped with the
southernwoods. *A. borealis* is lower than the others and
makes a compact shrubby perennial with very gray foliage. *A. glacialis* makes a 4-in. mound of fine gray leaves.

The southernwoods are propagated by cuttings in
spring or summer, or by removing side roots in spring.

Tarragon

French tarragon, *A. Dracunculus sativa,* is used for seasoning and in the making of vinegars.

The perennial grows to 2 ft. and is propagated by root division in spring or fall. Tarragon needs sun, good drainage, and fertilizer every year.

The Wormwoods

The most familiar of the artemisias, they grow large in the third or fourth year; the crown spreads, and the stems may go to 4 ft. The foliage is an interesting blue-gray, and the leaf shape is like that of chrysanthemum. Wormwood is a good accent. Its late tall flower heads are brown with yellow seeds. *A. absinthium,* the true wormwood, is a large gray shrublike herb that grows to 2 to 4 ft. *A. frigida,* the fringed wormwood, grows to 18 in. and makes a good gray accent. Early in the season it resembles 'Silver Mound' (*A. Schmidtiana nana*), but at maturity spikes grow to 2 ft. and are hung with yellow blossoms. Roman wormwood (*A. pontica*) is a delicate gray herb with a lacy look; it rarely blooms. Beech wormwood (*A. Stelleriana*) has a thick white leaf and grows in great patches.

In the past mugworts were thought to contain many medicinal properties; now they are used decoratively, but *A. frigida* and *A. Schmidtiana* do not dry well.

Wormwoods grow in sun or shade. Seeds are slow to germinate, but self-sown seeds furnish some sturdy plants in spring. Old clumps gradually die. Each autumn cut *A. pontica* to the ground, and it will grow back again to make a low border by frost. The gray hedge remains attractive through the winter. The roots need to be curbed sharply twice during the year. Very sharp drainage and sandy soil are required for *A. Stelleriana.* Cut the plant back and root the cuttings in vermiculite. Grow in large patches.

ASPERULA

Rubiaceae

Upon the first of May,
With garlands fresh and gay,
With mirth and music sweet,
For such a season meet,
They passe their time away.
—Old song

Description:

Sweet woodruff has long been loved for its fragrance and as an ingredient in May wine. It makes an attractive ground cover in shade. It carpets the forests in Germany with glossy yellow-green leaves. In May it is covered with tiny white flowers. The plant grows in clumps that are 15 in. in diameter and 8 in. high. The green plant has a mossy smell, but the dry leaves give off the sweet scent of spring.

Uses:

During the Middle Ages sweet woodruff was used as a medicine for cuts and wounds and in garlands for church decorations. Today it is used in white wine, jelly, potpourri, and wreaths.

Culture:

This herb grows best in a shady site where the soil is humusy, moist, and acid. It may be grown from seed if there is plenty of room for it to remain undisturbed for some time. It will spread rapidly once it is established. In shady spots it needs sharp cutting back to let air into the thick plants, particularly in humid weather.

31

K.B.

BORAGO

Boraginaceae

Here is sweet water and borage for blending,
Comfort and courage to drink at your will.
—Nora Hopper

Borage (*Borago officinalis*) gained great popularity from the belief that a tea brewed from it gave courage as well as flavor to the person who drank it. The French used the tea in treating feverish catarrhs. Gerard said, "A sirup concocted of the floures quieteth the lunatick person and leaves eaten raw do engender good blood."

Description:

Hardy annual, 1 to 3 ft. Leaves oval, 6 to 8 ins. long, blue-green, and covered with fine hairs. These occur first in a basal rosette, then a succulent, prickly stem rises and branches out. Flowers star-shaped, heavenly blue and pink or lavender.

Uses:

Pick young leaves and use in salads for their cool cucumber flavor. Float the flowers in cups of wine, using claret, fruit juice, gin, and sugar. To candy the flowers, cut fresh, dip in beaten egg whites, then in sugar, and dry.

Culture:

Sunny location with well-drained, moist soil. Sow seeds in late fall or early spring where they are to grow. Cut back frequently to keep borage in good condition. If some old plants are dug out of the bed in midsummer, self-sown seedlings will fill the gaps and provide a fresh crop for autumn.

33

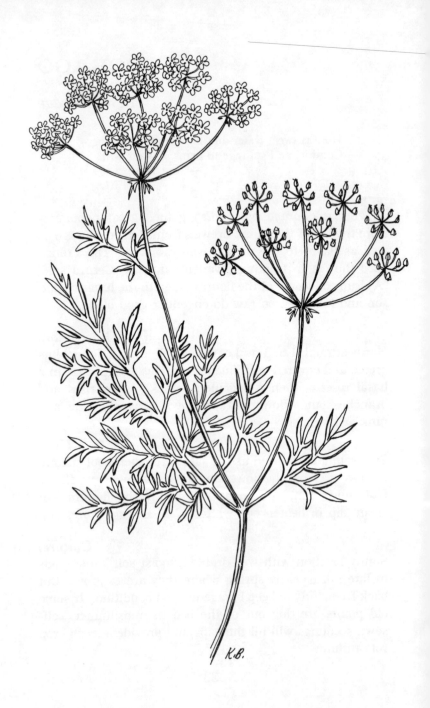

K.B.

CARUM

Umbelliferae

Nay, you shall see my orchard, where, in an
arbour we will eat a last year's pippin of
my own grafting, with a dish of caraways.
　　　　　　　　　—Shakespeare

Caraway(*Carum carvi*)seeds are reputed to strengthen
vision and to confer the gift of memory on all who eat
them. They were once thought to prevent the theft of any
object that contained them. Lovers were given the seeds
as a cure for fickleness, and pigeons were fed them to prevent their straying.

🕮 *Description:*
Hardy biennial, 1 to 3 ft. Furrowed stems with finely cut
leaves resembling the carrot's. Umbels of white flowers
in June of the second year.

🕮 *Uses:*
Caraway oil is extracted from the leaves and seeds. Young
leaves are sometimes used in soup; seeds, in applesauce,
apple pie, cookies, cakes and breads; the oil, in perfume,
soap, and in making a liqueur called kümmel; also to dis-
guise the taste of medicines and to stimulate digestion.
The thick, tapering roots, similar to parsnips but smaller,
are considered a delicacy for the table. Harvest the brown
crescent-shaped seeds before they fall to the ground and
before the birds begin to eat them, usually in August.

🕮 *Culture:*
Full sun and average, well-drained garden soil. Sow seeds
in September for an early spring crop of leaves and seeds
the following summer.

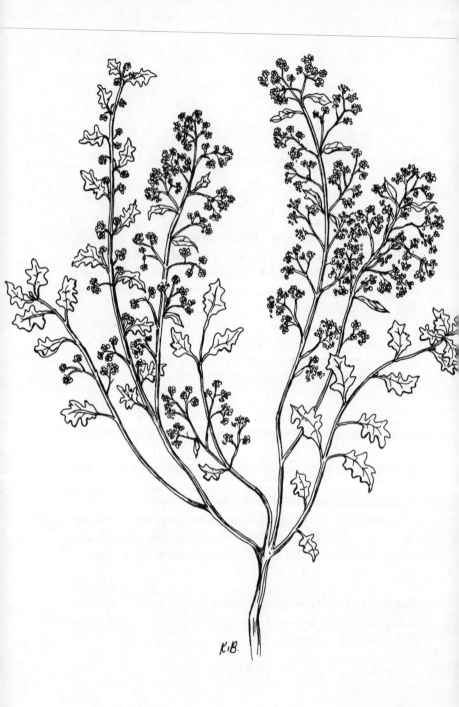

K.B.

CHENOPODIUM

Chenopodiaceae

Ambrosia was my mother's favorite, hence it is mine.
It was her favorite because she loved its pure spicy
fragrance. . . . This ever-present and ever-welcome scent
which pervaded the entire garden if leaf or flower
of the loved ambrosia be crushed, is curious and
characteristic, a true "ambrosiack odor" to use Ben
Jonson's words.

—Alice Morse Earle

Ambrosia (*Chenopodium botrys*) is known also as
Jerusalem oak and feather geranium.

🕮 *Description:*

Hardy annual, 2 ft., decorative and fragrant. Self-sown
seedlings appear in May with leaves like those of a small
oak tree. They are red on the back, dark green and marked like an oak on the top. As the plant grows, feathery
branches develop and the leaf-size diminishes. Sprays of
greenish flowers develop until, at maturity, the entire
plant looks like a lime-green plume.

🕮 *Uses:*

When branches have filled out to the seed stage, cut and
place in vases to dry naturally, without water. If kept out
of the sun, they will dry to a beautiful shade of green, wel-
come for fall and winter arrangements. Sprigs of ambrosia can be used in gin drinks as a flavoring.

🕮 *Culture:*

Full sun in sandy garden soil. Broadcast seeds over well-
prepared soil in fall or spring. Seedlings generally need
thinning; extras can be transplanted while they are still
small. Allow 12 ins. between seedlings. The most difficult
thing about ambrosia is that persons who do not know it
in the seedling stage mistake it for a weed.

CHRYSANTHEMUM

Compositae

Then balm and mint help to make up
My chaplet and for trial
Costmary that so likes the cup
And next it pennyroyal.
—Michael Drayton

Costmary (*Chrysanthemum balsamita* var. *tanace-toides*), also called alehost, is a native of the Orient now naturalized in our country. The French dedicated this herb to the Virgin Mary, but most of its associations have been with Mary Magdalene. Literature may refer to the plant as either St. Mary's herb or sweet Mary. The common name, "Bible leaf," came from Colonial times when it went to church as a marker for the Bible or prayerbook, but most of the pungent leaves were chewed on instead, during the endless sermons, as the minty flavor was supposed to keep the listener awake.

🕸 *Description:*
Hardy perennial, 2 to 3 ft., stiff stems with erect branches, short, and slightly downy. Leaves 6 to 8 ins. long with toothed margins. Flowers small, button-like, pale yellow, resembling tansy.

🕸 *Uses:*
Leaf as a bookmark; fresh or dry for tea and iced drinks. Place in closets and drawers, along with lavender, for a sweet odor.

🕸 *Culture:*
Thrives in well-drained soil and full sun, but will grow in semishade. Propagate by root division in spring or fall. Divide plants every third year.

39

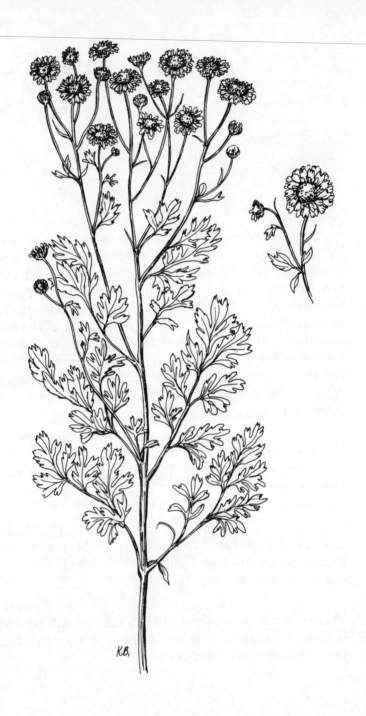

K.B.

CHRYSANTHEMUM

Compositae

There's many feet on this moor tonight,
And they fall so light as they turn and pass,
So light and true that they shake no dew,
From the featherfew and the hungry grass.
—Nora Hopper

Feverfew (*Chrysanthemum parthenium*) was named for its use in the treatment of fevers, but the showy white daisy flowers gave it a happier common name, "bride's button." In the past this plant was located close to dwellings because it was reputed to purify the atmosphere and to ward off disease. It was employed in the treatment of hysteria, nervousness, and lowness of spirits. A tincture made from feverfew warded off insects, and a wash of it was used to relieve the pain of insect bites.

Description:
Hardy perennial, 2 to 3 ft. Leaves light green with strong daisy-like odor. The inch-wide white daisies entirely cover the plants in June. If plants are cut back afterwards to maintain a neat appearance there will be some recurrent bloom later.

Uses:
In the perennial flower border and as a cut flower.

Culture:
Sun to partial shade in moist, well-drained soil. Sow seeds or set out plants in the early spring. Divide established plants every fall or spring, replanting only the strongest divisions.

41

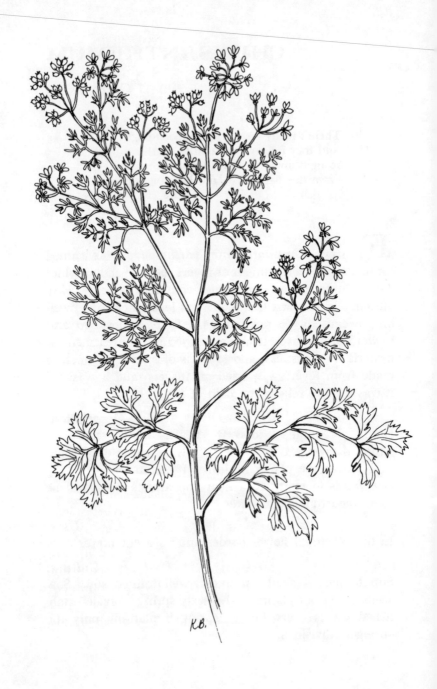

CORIANDRUM

Umbelliferae

And the manna was as coriander seed, and the colour thereof as the colour of bdellium.

Numbers 11:7

Coriander *(Coriandrum sativum)* is one of the earliest known spices: found in Egyptian tombs and used as a meat preservative in Rome. It came to England with the Romans and was cultivated in monastery gardens during the Middle Ages. Coriander was brought to America with the first colonists. It was used medicinally by the Egyptians and by Hippocrates. In *The Thousand and One Nights* coriander was used as an aphrodisiac and associated with fennel to summon devils.

℞ *Description:*
Annual, 2 ft. Leaves finely cut like parsley. Delicate flowers in umbels, rosy lavender, appearing in late June.

℞ *Uses:*
Harvest seeds as early as possible, otherwise they will bend the weak stems to the ground and be lost. Use in curry, in chopped meat, stews, sausage, gingerbread, cookies, and candies. The seed is very fragrant as well as flavorful and is often used in potpourri.

℞ *Culture:*
Full sun in well-drained, moist, and fertile soil. Sow seeds in early spring where they are to grow, and thin out the seedlings while they are still small. If not harvested promptly, the seeds will self-sow and spring up all around the parent plants.

K.B.

FOENICULUM

Umbelliferae

Above the lowly plants it towers,
The fennel with its yellow flowers,
And in an earlier age than ours
Was gifted with the wondrous powers
Lost vision to restore.
                —Henry Wadsworth Longfellow

Fennel (*Foeniculum vulgare*) was esteemed in ancient times as the herb to strengthen sight; and seeds, leaves, and roots were used for those "that are grown fat," wrote William Coles, "to . . . cause them to grow more gaunt and lank."

℞ *Description:*
Perennial sometimes grown as an annual, 4 to 5 ft. The stems are blue-green, smooth and glossy, flattened at base. Leaves bright green and feathery. Yellow flowers in umbels. Florence fennel (*F. vulgare* var. *dulce*), also called finocchio, has an enlarged leaf base which is cooked as a vegetable. The young stems of Sicilian fennel (*F. vulgare* var. *piperitum*) can be blanched and eaten like celery. Fennel varieties with bronze or copper foliage are preferred in the West because of their color, hardiness, perennial habits, and good flavor.

℞ *Uses:*
Tender leaves and stems in relishes, salads, and as a garnish. Use leaves for flavoring in fish sauces, soups, and stews; ripe seeds to flavor puddings, spiced beets, sauerkraut, spaghetti, soups, breads, cakes, candy, and alcoholic beverages.

℞ *Culture:*
Full sun in average garden soil. Propagate by sowing seeds in the spring after the soil is warm.

K.B.

GALIUM

Rubiaceae

Sleep, sweet little babe, on the bed I have spread thee;
Sleep, fond little life, on the straw scattered o'er,
'Mid the petals of roses, and pansies I've laid thee,
In crib of white lilies; blue bells on the floor.
                                    —Old Latin Hymn

Our Lady's bedstraw (*Galium verum*) is an herb said to have been present in the manger hay in Bethlehem where it made a bed for the Christ Child. In the reign of Henry VIII it was used as a hair dye. In Gerard's day it was an ointment and a foot bath.

🏵 *Description:*
Hardy perennial, 2 ft. Dainty foliage creeps along the ground in spring; later, as the yellow, fragrant blossoms develop in June, the plant grows taller until July, when the stems become stiff and dry. The small, slender leaves form whorls about the stems.

🏵 *Uses:*
As a filler in flower arrangements.

🏵 *Culture:*
Full sun to partial shade in average garden soil, even in unmanageable problem areas provided they are well-drained. Obtain plants and, after they become established and have multiplied, divide the roots in spring using the young offshoots. Water well and deeply until the roots take hold. This is a spreading plant and can crowd out weeds. If used as a ground cover, it may be cut back sharply and often to keep low, or allowed to grow until finished blooming, then cut back. Young plants of bedstraw bloom all through July and sometimes in the fall. This plant has become naturalized in the Berkshire Mountains of New England.

K.B.

HYSSOPUS

Labiatae

Purge me with hyssop, and I shall be clean:
wash me, and I shall be whiter than snow.
—Psalm 51:7

Hyssop *(Hyssopus officinalis)* was once considered a Bible plant, but recent research has proven that it was a native of Europe and not known in Palestine. Hyssop was once a remedy for quinsy and was used in treatments of colds and lung diseases. A decoction of it was supposed to remove bruises, and the oil was used in perfumes and liqueurs.

Description:
Hardy perennial, 1 to 1½ ft. Plant bears a slight resemblance to boxwood. Leaves narrow, small and pointed, dark green on woody stems. Flowers dark blue, pink, or white in spikes.

Uses:
Sometimes employed as a hedge, but some old plants die out annually and have to be replaced with strong seedlings. The flowers are excellent for cutting. Hyssop's culinary uses are largely in the past as its flavor and odor do not generally please contemporary tastes.

Culture:
Full sun, well-drained garden soil, rather alkaline. Seeds sown in well-prepared, moist soil in the spring germinate readily, becoming sturdy seedlings that transplant easily. If used as a hedge, plant a double row of seeds. Keep the main part of the hedge trimmed, but allow plants on the ends or in an out-of-the-way place to bloom so that self-sown seedlings can replace plants that die out.

49

LAMIUM

Labiatae

It makes the heart merry,
Drives away melancholy,
Quickens the spirits.
—Nicholas Culpeper

Lamiums have an interesting past as medicinal herbs, and today they make outstanding ground cover plants. *Lamium album,* the white dead nettle or white archangel, resembles the stinging nettle, but does not have its irritating disadvantages. In the past the flowers were baked in sugar, and a water distilled of them was said to make the heart merry, to give good color, and to make the vital spirits livelier. Tincture of the astringent plant was applied with cotton to stop bleeding. It was used also as a blood purifier and for eczema. *L. maculatum,* once called "cobbler's bench," has heart-shaped leaves marked with silver and spikes oᶜ white or light purple flowers. It is one of the most decorative of all ground covers, long-blooming, and the foliage stays attractive even after the first freezes of autumn. A prolific but not rampant ground cover.

🕸 *Description:*
Both species mentioned are hardy perennials.

🕸 *Uses:*
As showy ground cover plants where the attractive foliage sets off white or purple flowers depending on the variety.

🕸 *Culture:*
Partial sun to shade in good soil. Propagate by removing portions of the creeping stems which have rooted into the moist earth in spring or fall.

K.B.

LAURUS

Lauraceae

And when from Daphne's tree he plucks more Baies
His shepherd pipe may chant more heavenly lays.
—William Browne

Bay *(Laurus nobilis)* on its native shores of the Mediterranean grows to a majestic tree 60 ft. tall. The leaves, berries, and oil all have narcotic properties. Oil of bay is used for sprains, and the leaves were once used for a tea. Other plants called laurel, as our native *Kalmia latifolia,* cannot be used as bay. There are only two plants whose leaves are used as bay, *Laurus nobilis* and *Magnolia glauca.* Native laurels are poisonous and should not be used at all.

Description:
Tender perennial, 3 to 6 ft. when cultivated in a pot or large tub. Elegant, smooth-barked tree, evergreen leaves thick, smooth, and dark in color. Flowers small, in clusters, seldom appearing in the North.

Uses:
As an ornamental pot-grown tree for the garden in warm weather, for house or greenhouse during cold seasons. Use leaves for seasoning in stews, in casseroles, and pâtés.

Culture:
Propagate by rooting cuttings in moist sand and peat moss; provide shade and a moist atmosphere. Rooting may take six months or more. Suckers and cuttings from them root more quickly.

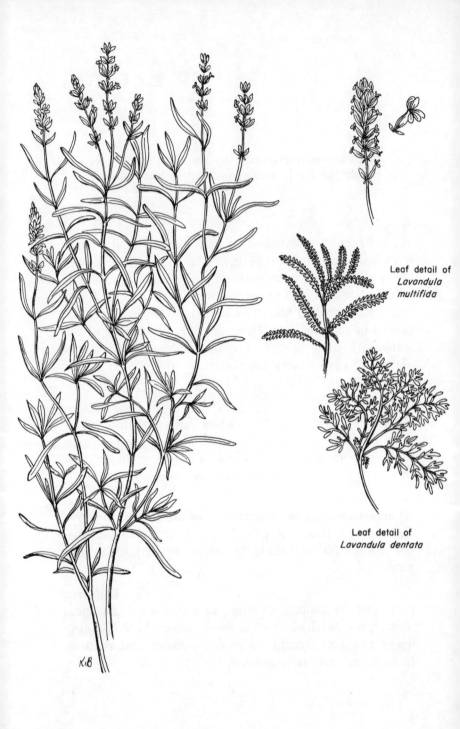

Leaf detail of
*Lavandula
multifida*

Leaf detail of
Lavandula dentata

K.B

LAVANDULA

Labiatae

Lavender is of especial good use for all griefes
and paines of the head and brain.
                    —John Parkinson

Lavender *(Lavandula officinalis)* came to England
with the Romans and found its happiest home there. It
was used by the Greeks and Romans much as we use it
today: for its clean sweet scent in washing water, soaps,
pomades, and perfuming sheets. It was a strewing herb
in medieval times and a medicine believed to cure 43
ills of the flesh and spirit. Lavender has always been
used to attract the bees and it produces an epicure's
honey.

℞ *Description:*
Hardy perennial, 1 to 3 ft. A woody semishrub that is
many-branched with narrow leaves, 1 to 2 ins. long, gray-
green and velvety. Flowers small and lavender, in whorls
of 6 to 10 on long-stemmed slender spikes. There are
small species and varieties that make fine ornamental
border plants; larger ones can be used for unclipped
hedges. Some tender kinds that grow well indoors are
discussed in Chapter 2.

℞ *Uses:*
Dried leaves and flowers in potpourri. Oil of lavender is
used in soaps and perfumes.

℞ *Culture:*
Sunny, well-drained, alkaline soil. Lavender can also be
propagated from slips with the heel attached, in moist
sand; July is a good time to do this.

K.B.

LEVISTICUM

Umbelliferae

An herb of the sun, under the sign Taurus,
if Saturn offend the throat . . . this is your
cure.

—Nicholas Culpeper

Lovage (*Levisticum officinale*) is a native of the Balkan countries, Greece, and other Mediterranean parts. It is one of the oldest salad herbs and was a favorite in colonial gardens. The English use it chiefly for confectionary: coating the seeds with sugar. Lovage was an ancient cure for ague; also for intestinal disorders.

Description:
Hardy perennial, 3 to 5 ft. A vigorous, coarse plant. Leaves dark green resembling celery in appearance, odor, and taste. Flowers small, greenish, in small umbels; not decorative. The plant turns yellow and unattractive in late summer.

Uses:
Harvest tender leaves for soups, stews, potato salad, salad greens, sauces. Blanch stems and eat as celery. The seeds, whole or ground, make cordials and may be used in meat pies, salads, and candies. Oil from the roots flavors some tobacco blends.

Culture:
Partial shade in fertile, deep, and evenly moist soil. May be propagated by division in spring, or from seeds, if they are sown in autumn immediately after they have ripened. Cover them lightly, and germination should occur the following spring.

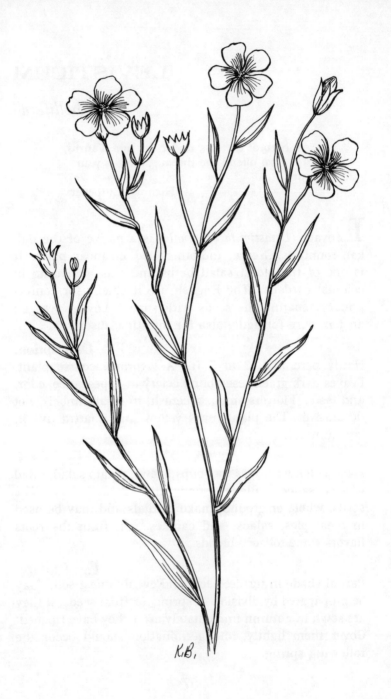

K.B.

LINUM

Linaceae

Flax (*Linum usitatissimum* and *L. perenne*), the source of linen and native to all Mediterranean countries, is a crop about which many legends have grown up. Both species have been used for linen, but the first mentioned is more important. The fresh herb was applied for rheumatic pains, colds, and coughs. Flax seed as a poultice softened hard swellings. If a baby did not thrive he was laid upon the ground in a flax field, flax seeds were sprinkled over him, and it was believed that he would recover as the seeds sprouted.

Description:
L. usitatissimum is an annual, 1 to 2 ft. It has slender blue-green leaves on willowy stems and bright blue flowers. *L. perenne* is a hardy perennial, to 2 ft. The blue flowers open with the sun, wither by noon. The blooms appear in June and July, but young plants frequently have another blossoming period in fall.

Uses:
For color in the herb garden.

Culture:
Both species like full sun. *L. usitatissimum* needs a rich, moist soil. *L. perenne* does better in a well-drained aklaline soil, and best perpetuates itself by reseeding in a soil made porous by gravel and rocks. Sow flax seeds in the spring where the plants are to grow.

LIPPIA

Verbenaceae

It grows along the old cathedral wall,
Where volcano shadows fall,
Herba Luisa of sweetest smell
Makes a tea as well.

—A. G. S.

Lemon verbena (*Lippia citriodora*), native to Central and South America, was long thought to be an herb of colonial gardens. Actually, it was one of the later arrivals in North America. Some say that the Spanish conquistadors took it back to Spain, and from there the plant spread through the south of Europe. In Latin America the lemon verbena is called *herba luisa,* and it is used for healing.

℞ *Description:*
Tender perennial, to 6 ft. as a tubbed plant. Leaves yellow-green indoors, glossy and darker outdoors. Flowers white and insignificant, borne infrequently.

℞ *Uses:*
Dry the leaves for potpourri and to steep for tea. Fresh leaves may be used to garnish salads, to make some jellies and desserts. The lemon verbena oil of commerce comes from another plant called lemon grass (*Cymbopogon citratus*).

61

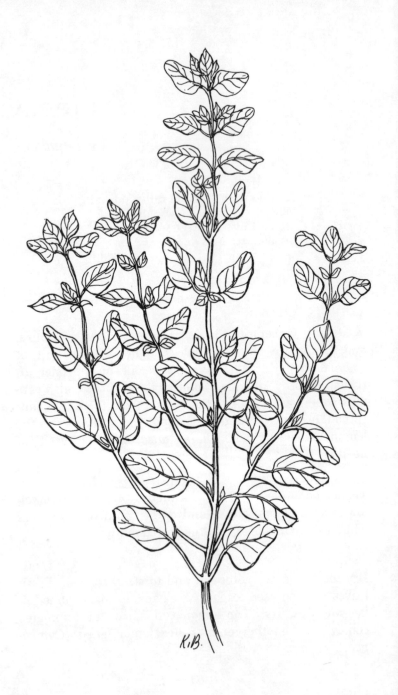

K.B.

MAJORANA

Labiatae

And though sweet Marjoram will your garden paint
With no gay colors, yet preserve the plant,
Whose fragrance will invite your kind regard,
When her known virtues have her worth declared;
On Simonis' shore fair Venus raised the plant,
Which from the Goddess touch derived her scent.
—René Rapin

Sweet marjoram (*Majorana hortensis*, sometimes listed as *Origanum majorana*) was used by the Greeks as a medicine for narcotic poisoning, convulsions, and dropsy. Because of its sweetness it was used also as a polish for furniture and as a strewing herb.

Description:
Tender perennial, grown as an annual in the North, to 1 ft. Leaves gray-green, rounded, and velvety. Flowers in white clusters like the blossoms of hops.

Uses:
Plants attractive in a border. Use fresh or dried leaves in soups, in stuffings for pork or lamb, and with eggs. The leaves may be used also in potpourri, and in English country places they are brewed into tea. Harvest the fresh leaves any time. Cut frequently to prevent blossoming. Wash well and hang up to dry overnight, then finish the drying process in a basket. Remove leaves when dry, crush, and store.

Culture:
Full sun in well-drained, alkaline soil. Sow seeds in carefully pulverized soil in the spring. Cover lightly with shredded sphagnum moss and keep moist. Germination may be slow. After transplanting seedlings, water well, and keep shaded until the roots take hold. Cuttings root easily.

63

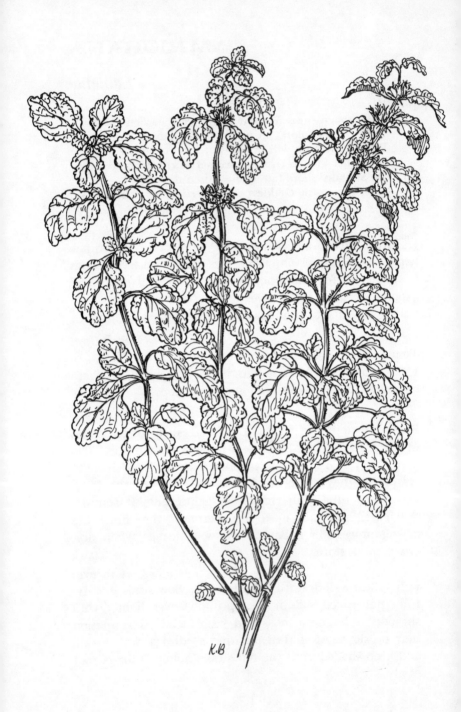

K.B

MARRUBIUM

Labiatae

Horehound is one of the five plants stated by the Mishna to be the "bitter herbs" which the Jews were ordered to take for the feast of the Passover.

—Richard Folkard

Horehound (*Marrubium vulgare*) has been used as a medicine since early Roman times. The Egyptians called it the seed of Horus, bull's blood, and eye of the star. It is an ancient antidote for vegetable poisons, and recommended by Gerard, "To those who have drunk poyson or have been bitten of serpents."

🕮 *Description:*

Perennial, only half-hardy in severely cold climates, to 2 ft. Leaves wrinkled and almost white, forming rosettes in early growth. In summer the plant branches out and puts on a burlike blossom. For best appearance keep the blooms cut off, although in this treatment you lose the self-sown seedlings that are useful in making living, autumn wreaths.

🕮 *Uses:*

As flavoring for famous horehound candy; as a tea to treat coughs and as a syrup for children's coughs and colds. The strange musky odor disappears upon drying.

🕮 *Culture:*

Full sun and sandy, dry soil. Except in mild climates, treat as a biennial, sowing a few seeds each year. Horehound can also be propagated by making cuttings in the spring or summer, or by dividing large plants in the spring. Interesting to try potted on a sunny cool window sill, or in a home greenhouse for the winter.

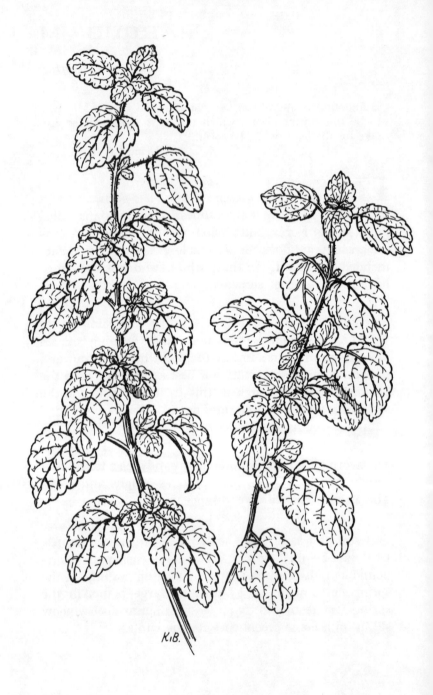

K.B.

MELISSA

Labiatae

The several chairs of order look you scour
With juice of balm and every precious flower.
—Shakespeare

Lemon balm (*Melissa officinalis*) came from the mountainous regions of southern Europe. Linnaeus named it *melissa*, the Greek word for bee, owing to the bees' attraction to the plant. Lemon balm was an ingredient of the famous Carmelite water, and in the past has been used along with honey as a potion to assure longevity.

₯ *Description:*
Hardy perennial, 1 to 2 ft., with branches growing on a square stem. Leaves broadly heart-shaped, toothed, 1 to 3 ins. long. Flowers inconspicuous, white or yellowish, off and on from June to October.

₯ *Uses:*
Makes an excellent mild tea. Good also for punch, for claret cup, fruit desserts, and as a garnish for fish. The oil is distilled and used in perfumery and also as a furniture polish. The dry leaves are used in potpourri.

₯ *Culture:*
Grows freely in any soil, but best in a well-drained location. Needs sun half a day, but will grow in shade. When plants are in a flower border, they need to be cut back to keep the foliage a good color as it has a tendency to turn yellow after flowering. Propagate by transplanting self-sown seedlings, or by sowing seeds (germination is slow).

67

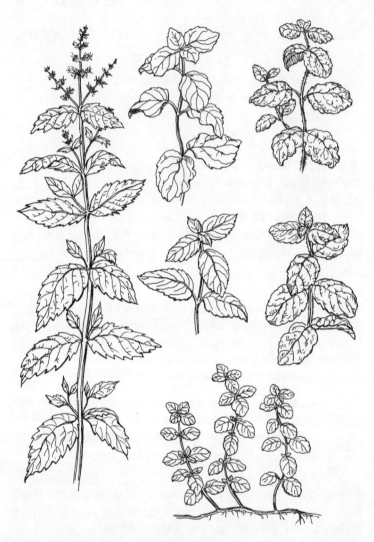

THE MINTS: (left) spearmint *Mentha spicata*, (top center) orange *M. citrata*, (top right) pineapple *M. rotundifolia variegata*, (middle) peppermint *M. piperata*, (middle right) apple *M. rotundifolia*, (bottom) pennyroyal *M. Pulegium*

MENTHA

Labiatae

Come buy my mint, my fine green mint!
Let none despise the merry, merry cries
of famous London town.
　　　　　　　—Old London street cry

The generic name *Mentha* was applied first by Theophrastus, a Greek philosopher-scientist and herbalist who
succeeded Aristotle as head of the Lyceum in 322 B.C.
In mythology Mintho was a nymph of great beauty who
was loved by Pluto, god of the underworld. Persephone
became jealous and changed the nymph into the fragrance of the mint. There are few plants in today's gardens as loved and as useful or as despised for their
rankness. In spring they look like hundreds of small
green roses opening to the world, and touching them
stirs up rich odors.

M. arvensis. The familiar red-stemmed mint that has
small green leaves and comes up late in spring. It has
a true spearmint flavor and is good for jelly and summer
drinks. It thrives in moist shade but will grow most
anywhere.

M. citrata. The bergamot or orange mint is treasured
for its fragrance and manageability. The dark-green
leaves are rounded, broad, and touched with purple.
Sometimes the undersides take on a deep shade of red;
in spring the whole plant is distinctly reddish purple.
As the season advances, leaves become green and ripe for
cutting. Fresh leaves may be used in punch and in summer flower arrangements. Harvest and dry leaves two or

three times during the summer for winter teas and pot-pourri. The leaves become well dried in a day and a night.

M. crispa. This curly mint has a spearmint flavor and a very waxy leaf. It grows to 2 ft. It is a rampant spreader and an excellent ground cover but needs to be cut back occasionally. It may be grown in a container. Pick it for bouquets and for garnishing cold drinks.

M. gentilis. Called apple mint because of its gold-flecked leaves. Dark-red stems rise from the earth late in spring. Its fine spearmint flavor is good in drinks.

M. niliaca. The Egyptian mint is a tall plant with woolly gray rounded leaves. It may grow to 5 ft., though it rarely goes over 3 ft. in the North. Use the leaves for tea, candying, and in arrangements.

M. piperita. English black peppermint is a handsome dark plant with almost black stems and leaves which creep along the ground in early spring and later grow up to 3 or 4 ft. It has beautiful dark purplish-blue flowers. Peppermint is vigorous but tends to die out if grown in the same place for several years; when it is grown commercially, the location is changed every second or third year. The plant is valued in commerce as a source of oil for medicine and seasoning.

M. Pulegium. Pennyroyal is a charming creeper. It forms a dense aromatic mat of glossy leaves, travels fast, and makes an excellent ground cover. The plant is not winter hardy, but it can be grown inside during the cold months. The best-known use of pennyroyal is warding off fleas. An infusion of the leaves is sometimes used for cramps, spasms, and colds, but it is very dangerous when consumed in large amounts.

M. Requienii. Corsican mint has the odor of crème de menthe, but a far less extravagant essence is used in the manufacture of the liqueur. It is minute and mossy and can be identified only by the odor. The plant has been grown in sun, but it thrives in shade, in well-drained and moist soil, and protected from drying winds. All the winter protection it needs is some sand on the small leaves.

M. rotundifolia. Apple mint has gray-green fuzzy leaves and gray-white blossoms that shade to pink or pale purple. Make at least three cuttings between June and October; use the tender leaves for teas, and candy some for cake decorations. Apple mint grows in either sun or shade and in either rich or lean soil. The tall growth makes an attractive cover for an unsightly spot, but it is very difficult to contain.

M. r. variegata. Pineapple mint is a small form (to 18 in.) of apple mint. The white-splotched leaves that vary with the seasons sometimes give the effect of flowers and make a fine garden accent. Although the plant has survived winter, it is safer to keep it in a cool spot in the house, in a window box or hanging basket, from autumn to spring. Root cuttings will grow in a window, a greenhouse, or a sheltered spot over winter. Use the leaves of pineapple mint to decorate jellied fruit desserts or fruit cups. It has little taste, but the odor is wonderful.

M. spicata. The famous spearmint is of easy culture and grows to 3 ft. tall. The leaves are excellent for iced tea, juleps, candy, salads, garnishing green peas, pea soup, sauces, and dried for tea, which is a general remedy for diarrhea and neuralgia. The tea is also used for washing wounds and sores.

🕭 *Culture:*
Mints will grow almost anywhere. They thrive in moist humusy soil, in shade but also in sun, and few pests ever bother them. The only problem with mints is that they spread too rapidly, overrunning other plants and growing into a mass instead of staying in neat separate clumps. To avoid this, plant each clump of mint in a metal barrel with top and bottom removed; sink it 18 in. into the ground. Or insert metal strips 12 to 18 in. deep around the plantings.

71

K.B.

MONARDA

Labiatae

Speak not, whisper not,
Here bloweth thyme and bergamot,
Softly on thee every hour
Secret herbs their spices shower.
    —Walter de la Mare

Beebalm (*Monarda didyma*), known also as bergamot and oswego tea, is one of the few native American herbs used in the garden.

       ℞ *Description:*
Hardy perennial, to 3 ft. Leaves 4 to 6 ins. long, dark green. Flowers in dense terminal clusters with reddish bracts, the color magenta, pink, purple, red, or white, depending on the variety.

           ℞ *Uses:*
Outstanding in the perennial border. The fragrant plants emit the characteristic odor of bergamot, similar to that of citrus. Use the leaves to make a tea, in potpourri, to flavor apple jelly, in fruit salads, and wine cups. Bergamot oil comes from a tropical tree, not from this plant, though the odors are similar. Bergamot flowers are excellent cut; long-lasting and effective in colonial arrangements.

          ℞ *Culture:*
Sun to partial shade in rich, evenly moist soil. Cut back after bloom as the foliage is sometimes unattractive in late summer. Propagate by division in spring or fall.

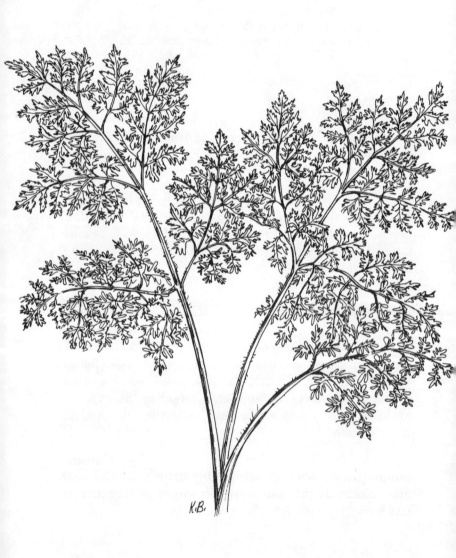

K.B.

MYRRHIS

Umbelliferae

Very good for old people who are dull
and without courage.
—Old Saying

Sweet cicely (*Myrrhis odorata*) has been known by
many common names including myrrh flower, sweet chervil, anise fern, and shepherd's needle. In history it has
been useful in treating coughs and as a gentle stimulant
and tonic for young girls. A decoction of the roots in wine
was taken for bites of vipers and mad dogs. An ointment
eased skin eruptions and the pains of gout.

🌿 *Description:*
Hardy perennial, 2 to 3 ft. The long thick root sends up
branching stems of fragrant, anise-scented leaves that
resemble the fronds of a delicate fern at maturity. These
are downy on the undersides and marked with white
spots. The white flowers which appear in late May and
early June are followed by seeds an inch long and dark
brown when ripe.

🌿 *Uses:*
The spicy seeds fresh and green in herb mixtures as a
spice. Use the leaves in salads or as a filling in pastries.
The roots may be eaten like fennel, raw or boiled.

🌿 *Culture:*
Shady, moist soil. To grow from seeds, plant in autumn
while the seeds are still fresh. Transplant to permanent
positions in the spring, allowing plenty of space for the
mature plants. An excellent plant for the shady flower
garden.

75

K.B.

NEPETA

Labiatae

If you set it, the cats will eat it,
If you sow it, the cats won't know it.
—Old Rhyme

Catnip (*Nepeta cataria*), known variously as catnip, catmint, and catnep, is a native of Europe, common in England, and an escapee from American gardens until now it is considered wild.

Description:
Hardy perennial, 2 to 3 ft. Sturdy stems, straight and similar to other mints, square and set with leaves 2 to 3 ins. long, downy, heart-shaped, green above, gray below. Flowers pale purplish in dense clusters on spikes. The plant is attractive to bees, almost irresistible to cats, and disliked by rats. Other species recommended for the garden include *N. mussini*, *N.* 'Six Hills Giant,' *N. grandiflora*, *N. macrantha* (blue flowers in spring), *N. nuda* and *N. reticulata*.

Uses:
Cats usually like dried leaves and blossoms better than fresh. A tea brewed from dried leaves may be used to soothe the nerves. All the nepetas are decorative, and they are remarkable in dry weather, continuing to bloom until fall if cut back after the first flowering.

Culture:
Sun or partial shade in sandy or rich soil. Catnip self-sows after it has become established. Propagate also by division of roots in spring or fall.

77

K.B.

OCIMUM

Labiatae

Madonna, wherefore hast thou sent to me
    Sweet basil and mignonette?
Embleming love and health, which never yet
    In the same wreath might be.
             —Percy Bysshe Shelley

Sweet basil (*Ocimum basilicum*)is the most common-
ly grown basil although there are many others in cultivation. All have a clovelike flavor and spicy odor, some more
pungent than others.

Description:
Annual, to 2 ft. Leaves 1 to 2 ins. long, shining dark
green and pointed. The flowers are white or purplish in
spikes. *O. crispum* from Japan is called lettuceleaf basil;
it is excellent in salads. *O. basilicum* 'Bush' forms a large
bush with lemon odor and taste; its variety *minimum* has
tiny leaves and, if spaced 4 ins. apart in a row, each plant
will grow like a small shrub. 'Dark Opal' has reddish-
purple foliage, striking in plantings with gray-foliaged
plants, and white or pink flowers.

Uses:
Leaves in salads, vinegars, spaghetti, soups, with meat,
game, fish, and tomato dishes. Excellent also in flower
arrangements. Harvest before the plants blossom; cut off
flower buds to keep plants producing all summer. Always
leave two leaves or a circle of leaves toward the base of
each branch; new tops will grow in a week.

Culture:
Sun to partial shade in average, but moist garden soil.
After the weather has warmed in the spring, sow seeds
where the plants are to grow.

K.B.

ORIGANUM

Labiatae

Where the bee can suck no honey, she leaves her
sting behind; and where the bear cannot find
origanum to heal his grief, he blasteth all other
leaves with his breath.
        —Beaumont and Fletcher

Oregano (*Origanum vulgare*), also called wild marjoram, comes from the early name "organy," because of
its use in hot bags as an application for rheumatic swellings. Gerard says, "Organy is very good against the wam-
bling of the stomacke."

℞ *Description:*
Hardy perennial, 2 ft. Leaves dull, gray-green, oval, with
stems often purple. Flowers pink, white, purple or lilac.
The most flavorsome oregano is a small-leaved, almost
trailing plant with white flowers. It is easily overrun by
the coarser types and needs to be kept separate and wintered inside.

℞ *Uses:*
Leaves, fresh or dried, in spaghetti sauce, sparingly in
salads, on tomatoes, in herb seasoning mixtures. Use
flowers fresh in summer arrangements or dried in winter
wreaths and bouquets.

℞ *Culture:*
Full sun and average garden soil, on the dry side and
always well-drained. Propagate by division of established
plants in the spring, by rooting cuttings, or by sowing
seeds. The seeds usually produce considerable variation.

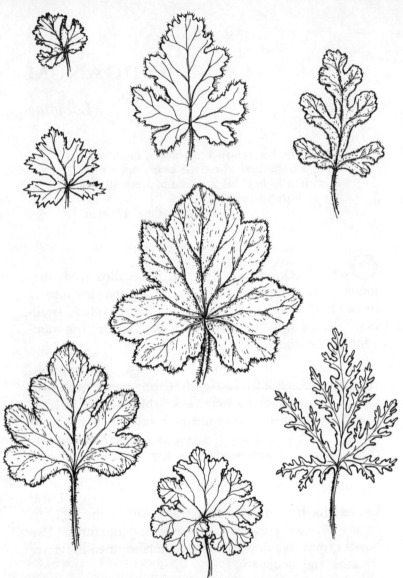

SCENTED GERANIUMS: (top left) lemon 'Prince Rupert' *Pelargonium crispum*, (middle left) strawberry *P. Scarboroviae*, (bottom left) P. 'Clorinda,' (top center) 'Attar of Roses' P. *capitatum*, (middle) peppermint P. *tomentosum*, (bottom center) 'Apple' P. *odoratissimum*, (top right) 'Staghorn Oak' P. *quercifolium*, (bottom right) lemon-rose P. Dr. Livingston or Skeleton Rose

PELARGONIUM

Geraniaceae

As aromatic plants bestow
No spicy fragrance while they grow,
But crush'd or trodden to the ground,
Diffuse their balmy sweets around.
—Oliver Goldsmith

The scented geraniums, members of the vast geranium family, are species and varieties of the genus *Pelargonium*, a word derived from the resemblance of their seedcases to a stork's bill. They give off a pleasing odor when they are brushed or crushed and yield a fragrant oil that may be distilled.

🦢 *Description:*
P. abrotanifolium 'Southernwood-leaved.' Pungent finely cut leaves resemble those of *Artemisia abrotanum.* Woolly stems are shrubby. Tiny blooms are white, the two upper petals each marked by a carmine dot.

P. blandfordianum. A tall plant with gray seven-lobed leaves which bears white flowers marked with carmine. Musky scent.

P. capitatum 'Attar of Roses.' The elusive rose scent is one of the world's most treasured. Attractive plant with light-green trilobate leaves and lavender blooms.

P. 'Clorinda.' Vigorous plant of trailing growth has large crenate, trilobate leaves that are rough textured and dusty green. Scent described as like eucalyptus or wild roses. Brilliant pink blossoms appear in abundance over a long period. Flourishes in terracotta tubs when watered and fertilized. Leaves turn red and some branches become bare when neglected; plant fills out again when watered.

P. crispum. A lemon geranium with a fragrance second only to that of *P. graveolens.* Small ruffled and fluted leaves grow on stiffly upright stems like pyramidal evergreens with orchid-pink flowers. Grow in tubs.

P. c. 'Gooseberry-leaved.' Ruffled leaves are mottled yellow. Useful in the foreground of a bed or window box. Upper petals of abundant pale-lavender flowers are lined with cerise. Propagation difficult.

P. c. 'Prince Rupert.' Like an upright little evergreen. Will become a small shrub during one summer in the garden. Plant in terracotta tubs and allow to grow as large as it will. One of the showiest plants for the pot garden; sturdy and strongly lemon-scented.

P. c. 'Prince Rupert Variegated.' A distinguished plant. The leaf is ruffled and green and creamy white. Usually remains small. Mild lemon scent.

P. denticulatum. Finely cut leaves form a dense plant with small lavender flowers. Rose-scented.

P. 'Dr. Livingston.' Skeleton-leaf rose geranium, vigorous, with a fragrance sometimes described as lemon, sometimes as rose. A handsome plant with light-green foliage and tiny pale-lavender flowers.

P. filicifolium. Sometimes called fernleaf geranium because of its finely cut leaves. A novelty for collectors. Leaves are sticky, with a pungent scent that is unpleasant to many. Tiny pink flowers have carmine marks. Tall and spreading.

P. fragrans 'Nutmeg.' Highly scented plant does well where small gray-green leaves can trail over pots or as edgings for geranium beds. Cut tops to border height.

P. glutinosum 'Pheasant's Foot.' Deeply cut brown-marked leaf shaped like a bird's foot. Vigorous; grows rapidly and makes a handsome background in bed or box.

P. graveolens. Large, with deeply cut gray-green foliage and lavender blooms. Grows to 3 to 4 ft. if not cut back. Leaves are good for jellies and teas. Rose-scented.

P. g. camphoratum or 'Camphor Rose.' Succeeds in being both camphorous and rosy. Leaf is velvety, pleasing to the touch, and bewitching to the nose.

P. g. 'Gray Lady Plymouth.' The best of the variegated rose geraniums. Vigorous; excellent for pots or beds. Leaf like that of *P. graveolens* with white border. Rose-scented.

P. g. 'Lady Plymouth.' Slow growing but reaches tremendous size. *Graveolens*-like leaf, but larger; light green with strong rose odor.

P. g. 'Little Gem.' This small rose geranium flowers freely. Interesting border plant. Pungent.

P. g. minor or 'Little Leaf Rose.' Very small *graveolens*-like leaves. Compact plant is covered with small orchid blooms in spring and early summer. Pungent.

P. g. 'Rober's Lemon Rose.' Sweetest of the rose scents. Long thick leaf is cut like tomato leaf. Vigorous plant yields hundreds of leaves for potpourri or tea.

P. g. 'Variegated Mint-scented Rose.' Gray-green leaves are deeply lobed and edged with creamy white. Use where foliage can be seen. Combined odor of mint and rose.

P. grossularioides 'Cocoanut.' A trailing plant with slender stems growing out of a crown of larger leaves. Tiny lavender blooms. The odor is pungent and delightful to some. Self-sows.

P. 'Joy Lucille.' This favorite for window boxes has deeply cut feltlike leaves on trailing stems. Good for edging containers. Scent described as peppermint or lilac.

P. Limoneum 'Lemon.' Fan-shaped toothed leaves have strong lemon scent. Variety 'Lady Mary' has delicate lemon scent and attractive magenta blossoms.

P. melissinum 'Lemon Balm.' Rapid-growing plant is important where height is needed. Plant has odor like lemon balm (*Melissa officinalis*), a light-green maple-like leaf, and small lavender flowers. It can be wintered over with a little light and water to keep it from shriveling.

P. 'Mrs. Kingsley.' The leaves, like curly parsley, are pungent with a hint of mint. Showy red flower.

P. nervosum 'Lime-scented.' Very fragrant and refreshing lime odor. Compact plant with small dentate leaves and lavender flowers.

P. odoratissimum 'Apple.' Light-green oval leaves, crenate and velvety, on vinelike branches, with tiny white flowers in spring. It is wonderful for windowsills or outdoors. Alternate it with *P. o.* 'Nutmeg' along a walk. It is trim and apple-scented.

P. 'Old Scarlet Unique.' Attractively cut leaves are very ruffled, often with a red edge, and are woolly and grayish. Scarlet flowers over long season. Pungent.

P. 'Old Spice.' Also known as 'Logee' and *P. logeei.* A sweetly scented trailing plant with small white flowers.

P. 'Prince of Orange.' Compact, with small crenate leaves, orange odor, and fine pale-orchid blooms.

P. quercifolium 'Beauty.' Mint-scented. Rough-textured oak-type leaves with brown markings. Excellent where large-leaved trailing plant is needed. Tiny rose flowers touched with purple.

P. q. 'Fair Ellen.' Round-lobed rough leaves and stems of trailing plant are sticky. Abundant lavender flowers of medium size. Pungent.

P. q. giganteum 'Giant Oak.' Three- to five-lobed leaves, large and coarse, marked in the veins with deep purple. Rangy growth, with sticky stems and leaves. Small rose flowers. Often trained to tree or standard forms and as a background. Not useful in small quarters.

P. q. pinnatifidum 'Sharp-toothed Oak.' Leaves are larger than those of 'Fair Ellen,' elongated, strikingly marked in purple, crinkled, five lobed, and very pungent. Attractive pale-pink flowers.

P. q. prostratum 'Prostrate Oak.' Excellent trailing plant, low and spreading. Five-lobed leaf with purple markings. Small lavender flowers. Pungent.

P. q. 'Skelton's Unique.' A rambling plant that covers a wall in a season, spreading in all directions for 5 to 6 ft. Small orchid blooms in spring and summer. Ruffled scalloped leaf has a dark, almost purple, center with tiny hairs that give a downy look. Pungent, with a hint of rose.

P. q. 'Staghorn Oak.' Finely cut leaf has purple veins. Choice trailer for containers. Blooms well.

P. q. 'Village Hill Hybrid.' One of the most important oak-leaved geraniums. Narrow crenate leaf. New leaves look like parsley. Bright-lavender flowers with purple veins. Grows quickly; almost climbs.

P. 'Rollinson's Unique.' A good climber to cover a wall. Grows 5 to 6 ft. in one season. Leaves slightly crinkled, mint-scented. Flowers brilliant magenta.

P. scabrum 'Apricot.' Handsome, with a dark-green glossy leaf. Pungent odor, with a hint of apricot. Large rose-colored flowers with deeper markings.

P. 'Shottesham Pet.' Most desirable pot plant. Beautiful shimmering-green lacy foliage. Numerous brilliant-pink blooms over a long season. Filbert-scented.

P. 'Shrubland Rose.' Attractive heavy glossy foliage on a vigorous plant that grows tall and spreads. Pungent. Lovely rose-colored blooms appear freely.

P. tomentosum. A shrubby plant with downy grapelike leaves. White flowers have a red spot near center. Tolerates light shade. Good for window boxes. Peppermint-scented.

P. torento 'Ginger.' Fan-shaped rounded leaves with brilliant rose-lavender flowers. Tall, rapidly growing plant needs to be cut back frequently. Pungent, with a hint of ginger.

℞ *Uses:*

Grow scented geraniums for fragrance and interesting foliage and flowers. Rose geraniums are good for tea, for use in potpourri, and for making rubbing alcohol. They are also used in jelly, for making sugars, and in many dessert recipes.

℞ *Culture:*

Scented geraniums are grown in containers, indoors or out, and need all the sunlight possible each day, evenly moist soil that is allowed to get dry only occasionally, and coolness in winter (72 degrees maximum). Remove yellowing leaves regularly to prevent the spread of disease. Many of these plants also do well in hanging baskets.

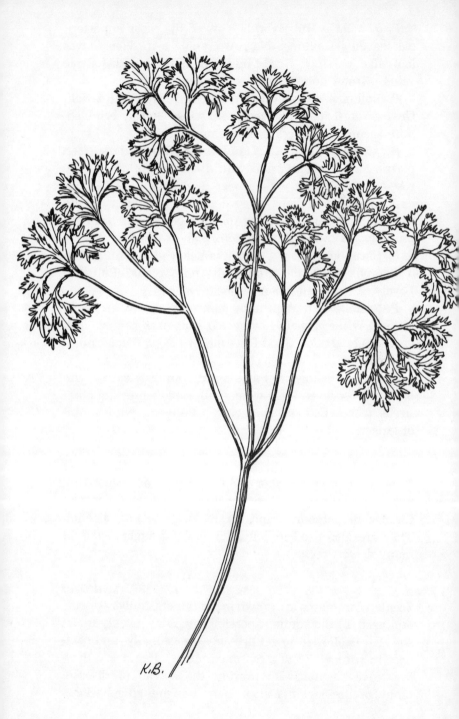
K.B.

PETROSELINUM

Umbelliferae

At Sparta's Palace twenty beauteous mayds,
The pride of Greece, fresh garlands crowned their heads
With hyacinths and twining parsley drest,
Graced joyful Menelaus' marriage feast.
—Theocritus

Parsley (*Petroselinum crispum*) is one of the first plants used in wreath making. Chaplets of it were worn at Roman and Greek banquets to absorb the fumes of the wine and thus prevent inebriation. Parsley was eaten after dining to remove the odor of garlic and onions, proving that our twentieth-century exploitation of chlorophyll as a breath-sweetener is nothing new.

Description:
Curly parsley is a hardy biennial usually cultivated as an annual. It has bright green, tightly curled leaves and makes an excellent border for the culinary garden. Italian parsley, also a hardy biennial cultivated as an annual, has large plain leaves reminiscent of a fern which may be cut in quantity for salad greens, or cooked as a vegetable.

Uses:
Cut all through the season, using generously in salads, soups, casseroles, and omelettes with other vegetables.

Culture:
Full sun or partial shade in humusy, moist soil. To grow from seeds, broadcast or plant in shallow drills in well-prepared soil. Sow in midsummer for autumn cutting and to have small plants to bring inside for winter window boxes; for an early summer crop, sow seeds in earliest spring.

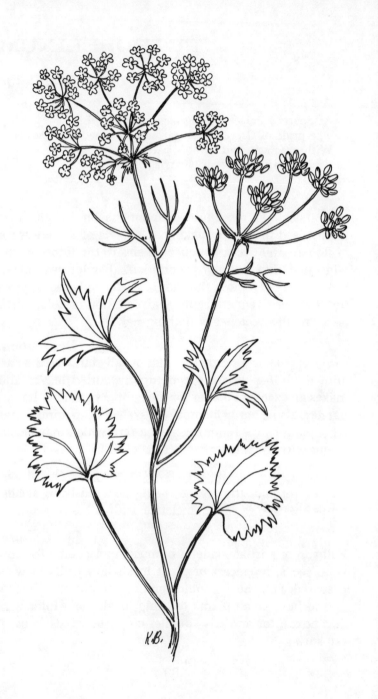

K.B.

PIMPINELLA

Umbelliferae

... for ye pay tithe of mint, and anise, and cummin ...
—Matthew 23:23

Anise (*Pimpinella anisum*) was used as a spice in Roman times and was the chief flavoring of the *mustacae*, cakes made of meal and filled with anise, cumin, and other flavorings. This was eaten to prevent indigestion and may be a forerunner of our wedding cake. The seed of anise was thought to avert the evil eye, and in Biblical lands it was used in payment of taxes. The oil has been used as mouse bait.

Description:
Annual, 1 to 1½ ft. Leaves finely cut, gray-green. Flowers white, small, in an umbel about 2 ins. across. The seeds are light-colored, crescent-shaped, with a small piece of stem that clings to them after harvesting.

Uses:
Watch plants carefully after flowers form to insure harvesting the seeds before they ripen and fall to the ground. When the seeds are fully formed, cut heads into a paper bag. Use as flavoring for cakes, cookies, candies, applesauce, stews, liqueurs, and wines, and use to impart fragrance to soaps, perfumes, and potpourri. Use fresh anise leaves in salads as a garnish.

Culture:
Sunny, well-drained soil enriched by the addition of compost. Sow the seeds very early in spring.

91

K.B.

ROSMARINUS

Labiatae

Young men and maids do ready stand
With sweet Rosemary in their hands—
A perfect token of your virgin's life.
    —Old Ballad (Roxburghe Collection)

Rosemary (*Rosmarinus officinalis*) is the herb of memory which it is said to restore, and it also brings good luck, prevents witchcraft, disinfects the air, and has been used traditionally at weddings and funerals.

** *Description:***
Tender perennial, 3 to 6 ft. There are many variations, but all are considered forms of common rosemary. The needle-like leaves vary in color from gray-green to dark green; some are shiny, broad, or very narrow. All are thick and without stems, gray or white on the undersides. The blossoms may be white-rose, pale lavender, pale or dark blue.

** *Uses:***
Green or dried, sparingly on chicken, in gravy with lamb, in soups, stuffings, sauces, dressings, in jelly, and as a tea. Rosemary oil is used in medicine, perfumes, hair preparations, bath soaps, and mouth washes.

** *Culture:***
Full sun to partial shade with evenly moist, well-drained, and alkaline soil. Provide liquid fertilizer several times during the active growing season. Root cuttings in sand or vermiculite using 4- to 6-inch pieces of new wood or healthy end tips. Seeds are not difficult, but are usually slow to germinate and require three years to bloom.

RUMEX

Polygonaceae

Sorrel sharpens the appetite, assuages heat,
cools the liver and strengthens the heart; . . .
in the making of sallets imparts a grateful
quickness to the rest as supplying the want of
oranges and lemons. Together with salt, it gives
both the name and the relish to sallets from the
vapidity, which renders not plants and herbs only,
but men themselves pleasant and agreeable.
    —John Evelyn

French sorrel (*Rumex scutatus*) is a native of southern France, Switzerland, and Germany. Historically its uses have been largely culinary, although it is alleged to "cool any inflamation and heat of the blood—a cordial to the heart." It was thought to be a source of iron and was once called "cuckoo's meate" because the bird was supposed to clear its singing voice by eating it.

🙿 *Description:*

Hardy perennial, 2 ft. Resembles the related and common dock of the fields. Leaves succulent, long and shield-shaped, light green in color, sometimes veined with red. Flowers like dock but smaller, softer in appearance, and a warm red-brown color.

🙿 *Uses:*

In sorrel soup, sparingly in salads, as a sauce for beef, or cooked with beet tops, spinach, or cabbage. Cut early in the spring and freeze some leaves for use later in the year. If allowed to blossom, use the flowering heads in dried arrangements. Cut to ground after harvest to encourage new growth for a fall crop.

🙿 *Culture:*

Sun to partial shade in rich, well-drained soil. Buy a plant, then allow it to multiply. Difficult to obtain seeds of the true variety. Broadleaf garden sorrel is a good substitute.

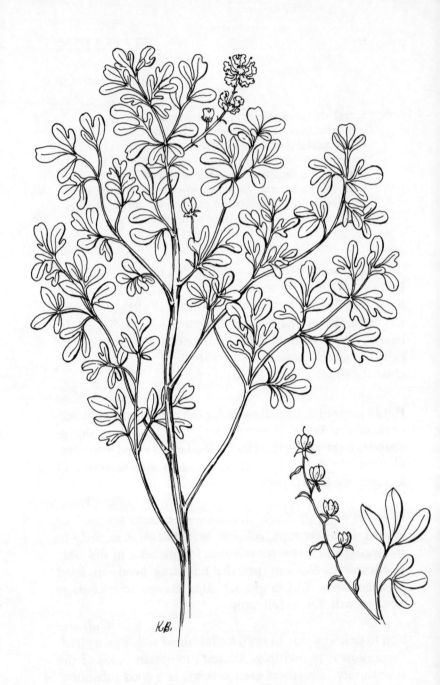

K.B.

RUTA

Rutaceae

Then sprinkled she the juice of rue,
That groweth underneath the yew,
With nine drops of the midnight dew
From lunarie distilling.
—Michael Drayton

Rue (*Ruta graveolens*), also called sweet rue and herb of grace, was once used to treat many diseases. It was said to bestow second sight, to preserve vision, and was used against old age and stiffening joints. Holy water was sprinkled with sprigs of rue, hence the name "herb of grace." Arrows supposedly found their mark after being dipped in the juice of rue, and rue is still used in Lithuania as a courting herb to announce engagements.

Description:
Hardy perennial, 3 ft. Leaves alternate, blue-green, musky smelling, much divided and notched on erect, stout woody stems. Yellow flowers that resemble a cluster of stars are followed by red-brown seed pods that look hand carved.

Uses:
As an ornamental plant toward the back of the border where it will have little opportunity to cause skin irritations, for which it is known, but where the foliage, flowers, and seed heads can be enjoyed. The dried seed heads are excellent for use in wreaths and swags.

Culture:
Full sun to partial shade in average garden soil, preferably dry, stony, and alkaline. Propagate by dividing old plants in late spring or, after blooming, by rooting cuttings or sowing seeds.

97

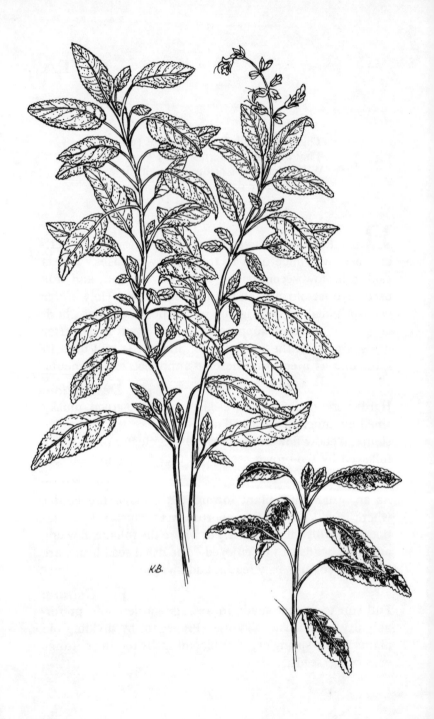

K.B.

SALVIA

Labiatae

Sage is singularly good for the head and the brain; it quick-
eneth the senses and the memory; strengtheneth the sinews;
restoreth health to those that hath the palsy; and takes away
shaky trembling of the members.

—John Gerard

Common sage (*Salvia officinalis*), in history, has been
the herb of health and of the aged. An old French couplet
expresses these virtues well, "Sage helps the nerves and
by its powerful might Palsy is cured and fever put to
flight." The Chinese once used it in preference to their
own teas, and employed it medicinally for headaches.
The fresh leaves were once used to strenghten the gums
and to whiten teeth; also it was used as a wash to darken
gray hair.

Description:
Hardy perennial, 3 ft. Leaves oblong, gray and pebbly, on
stiff stems that become woody and gnarled with age.
Flowers blue in whorls with lipped corollas that tempt the
bees and hummingbirds.

Uses:
Cut leaves of common sage at any time for cheese sand-
wiches, soufflés, and stuffings. Use dried in sausages,
with cheese, pork, poultry, as stuffing seasoning in turkey,
and as a tea.

Culture:
Sunny site with moist, well-drained garden soil. Seeds of
common sage sown in early spring will produce fine plants
for cutting by fall. Propagate in spring or early fall by
dividing old plants.

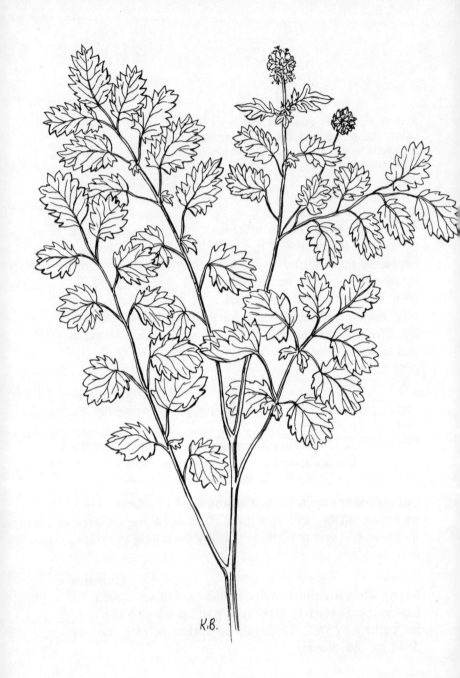

K.B.

SANGUISORBA

Rosaceae

But those which perfume the Aire most delightfully, not passed by as the rest, but being Trodden upon and Crushed, are Three: That is, Burnet, Wilde-Time, and Water-Mints. Therefore, you are to set whole Allies of them, to have the Pleasure, when you walke or tread.

—Francis Bacon

Salad burnet (*Sanguisorba minor*), of Mediterranean origin, then naturalized in England and Asia, came to America with the Pilgrims. As a cordial, it was used to promote perspiration, and infused in wine and beer it became a cure for gout.

Description:
Hardy perennial, 1 to 2 ft., evergreen. Leaves bear a similarity to those of the wild rose and remain nearly flat on the ground until flowering time. Flowers deep, but pale crimson in a round head.

Uses:
Fresh leaves smell of cucumber and may be cut while tender for salads, vinegars, cream cheese, drinks, seasoning green butters, and as a garnish. They do not dry well. Keep some plants close to the house, sheltered in a cold-frame or in a cool greenhouse, to provide winter greens.

Culture:
Sun with well-drained, alkaline soil. Sow seeds in late fall, early spring, and summer to have tender salad greens all year. Difficult to transplant except as a small seedling. This is one of the most decorative of herbs, worthy of space in most gardens.

101

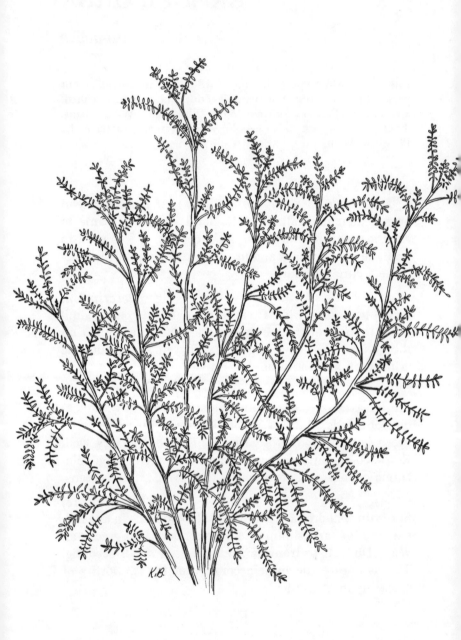

SANTOLINA

Compositae

White Satten groweth pretty well, so doth Lavender-Cotton.
—John Josselyn

Lavender-cotton (*Santolina chamaecyparissus*) is one of the most ornamental of all herbs. It is a native of southern Europe and North Africa.

🕸 *Description:*
Hardy perennial, 1 to 2 ft. Leaves very fine, yet sturdy; gray to white at certain seasons, but blue-gray while young. Flowers, few, globular and yellow, best trimmed off for neatness. *S. viridis* is a vigorous green santolina with a strong odor and interesting bright yellow flowers.

🕸 *Uses:*
For borders, especially in the knot garden, and as accent plants when grown in clumps.

🕸 *Culture:*
Full sun and average garden soil, dry or moist but perfectly drained. Propagate by rooting cuttings in sand or vermiculite. Transplant rooted cuttings into small pots until they make balls of roots, then move into the garden. Cut tops back to make plants bush out. Santolina is hardy in central and southern New England, considered half-hardy in the Berkshires, and must be covered in any area if it is to look presentable in the spring. Trim carefully in the fall as santolinas do not die to the ground but come out along the old wood.

103

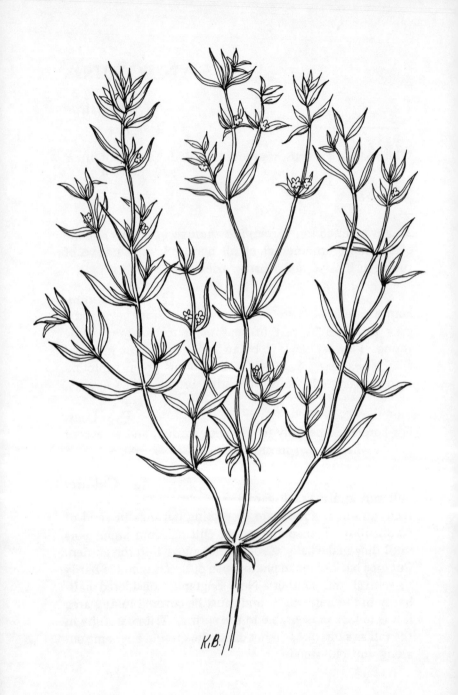

K.B.

SATUREJA

Labiatae

Mercury claims dominion over this herb.
Keep it dry by you all the year, if you
love yourself and your ease.
                    —Nicholas Culpeper

Summer savory (*Satureja hortensis*) is a Mediterranean native. Virgil grew savory for his bees, and the Romans used its hot peppery flavor before Eastern spices were widely known. Vinegar flavored with savory was used as a dressing and sauce.

🦋 *Description:*
Annual, 1 to 1½ ft. Leaves narrow, dark green, on stout stems that become branched and treelike in late summer, turning reddish and purple in fall. Flowers pale lavender or pure white, sometimes with a pink cast, covering the plant like drops of dew in July.

🦋 *Uses:*
Cut two or three times during the drying season, preferably before the blossoms form. Leave some to mature, but harvest for good green color from non-blooming plants. Hang to dry in a warm, dry place. Pull leaves off —a long task—make sure they are chip dry and store in bottles. Use in cooking green beans, for all bean dishes, in stuffings, with rice, in soups, gravies, and sauces.

🦋 *Culture:*
Sunny location in well-drained garden loam. Sow seeds in early spring, allowing about four weeks for germination. Broadcast in a wide, well-prepared row. Mulch with salt hay to prevent weeds and to keep leaves clean for cutting.

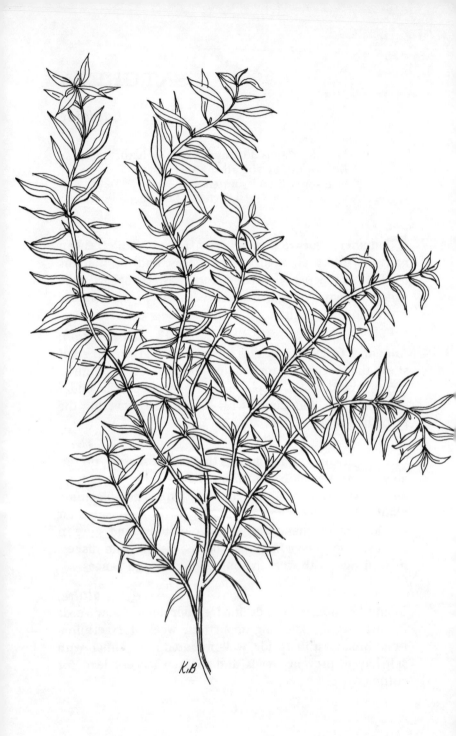

K.B

SATUREJA

Labiatae

Sound savorie, and brazil, hartie-hale,
Fat Colwortes and comforting Perseline,
Cold Lettuce and refreshing Rosmarine.
—Lady Northcote

Winter savory (*Satureja montana*) is a native of the
mountainous regions of southern Europe.

℞ *Description:*
Hardy perennial, 6 to 12 ins. Leaves narrow on branches
that form a low, spreading growth. Flowers either white
or blue. This is a good border plant, but at its best when
planted in a wall garden. *S. m. pygmaea* is dwarf, about
4 ins. tall, and highly to be recommended.

℞ *Uses:*
Harvest as for summer savory. Use in cooking green
beans, other bean dishes, in stuffings, with rice, in soups,
gravies, and bouquet garni. Winter savory, too, with basil
is a substitute for salt and pepper in salt-free diets. Used
occasionally in salad dressings. Winter savory was once
a proper dressing for trout. The leaves can be made into
a peppery-tasting tea.

℞ *Culture:*
Sunny, perfectly drained soil, on the lean side. Propagate
by hilling up an established plant with humusy, moist soil.
New plants will be ready to separate in four to six weeks.

K.B.

STACHYS

Labiatae

He has as many virtues as Betony.
—Spanish Saying

Lamb's-ear (*Stachys olympica*, or sometimes *S. lanata*), a native of the Caucasus, and bishop's wort (*S. grandiflora* syn. *betonica*) from Europe and Asia Minor were once classified with the betonys. The whole plants were collected for a flavorful tea, said to have all the good qualities of China tea plus virtues of its own. Betony was once thought to sanctify those who carried it.

Description:
Hardy perennials, *S. olympica* to 1 ft., *S. grandiflora* to 3 ft. *S. olympica* leaves are long-stemmed and linear, heavily covered by white "lamb's" hairs that give the plant a beautiful silvery appearance. Flowers purple, in spikes. *S. grandiflora* leaves are rough, covered with short hairs, and filled with oil that gives off an odor at a touch. Most of the elongated heart-shaped leaves spring from the root, large and on long stalks. The flower stems rise 1 to 3 ft. with pairs of leaves set on opposite sides of the stems. Flowers purplish red, in whorls on the spikes, in July and August.

Uses:
For flower arrangements and as showy border plants.

Culture:
Sunny with moist, well-drained soil. Propagate by division of established plants in spring or fall.

109

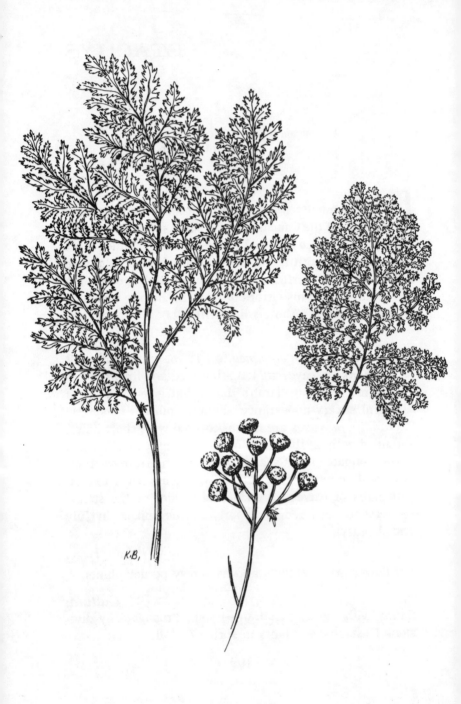

K·B,

TANACETUM

Compositae

On Easter Sunday be the pudding seen
To which the Tansy lends her sober green.
—*The Oxford Sausage*

Tansy (*Tanacetum vulgare*) has been called such names as bitter buttons, *herbe St. Marc,* and *Chrysanthemum vulgare.* It was once used as a bitter tea to bring out measles, also in tansy cakes for Easter festivities in England, and in New England coffins as a preservative—or as a symbol of immortality from its ancient use by Greeks and Romans at burials. It was believed effective for keeping away ants and flies, and the large leaves were kept in many colonial pantries for this purpose.

Description:
Hardy perennial, 3 ft. Attractive plant with coarse fernlike leaves. Flowers like yellow buttons in clusters. The variety *crispum,* or fernleaf tansy, is smaller and better for cultivated gardens.

Uses:
Dry the flowers as everlastings for fall and winter arrangements, wreaths, and swags.

Culture:
Sun to partial shade in almost any soil provided it is not wet for long periods. The chief problem with this plant is keeping it from becoming a weed, but if you should want to propagate it, do so by dividing well-established plants. Tansy is best when planted against a fence that will give it some protection from high winds and rains.

111

K.B.

TEUCRIUM

Labiatae

I like also little heaps in the Nature of the Mole Hills (such are in wilde Heaths) to be set some with Wilde-Time; Some with pincks; some with Germander, that gives a good flower to the eye.

—Francis Bacon

Germander (*Teucrium lucidum*) provided the basis of an ancient treatment for gout. Emperor Charles V is the most famous person to have been cured by this remedy. He took a decoction of the herb for sixty days in succession. It is native of the Greek islands.

🕮 *Description:*
Hardy perennial, 1 to 1½ ft. This plant lends itself to clipping as a small hedge and resembles boxwood. The leaves are small, stiff, and glossy dark green, the edges toothed. Flowers magenta, but best kept cut off so that the plants will stay bushy and full as a hedge. *T. chamaedrys* is hardier, almost a creeping plant, with leaves that turn reddish in fall or when the soil is dry. It makes a good ground cover for dry places and has rosy flowers.

🕮 *Uses:*
As small hedge for the perennial border or herb garden.

🕮 *Culture:*
Sun in well-drained, moist garden loam. Propagate by rooting cuttings early in the growing season. Cover with salt hay in the wintertime.

113

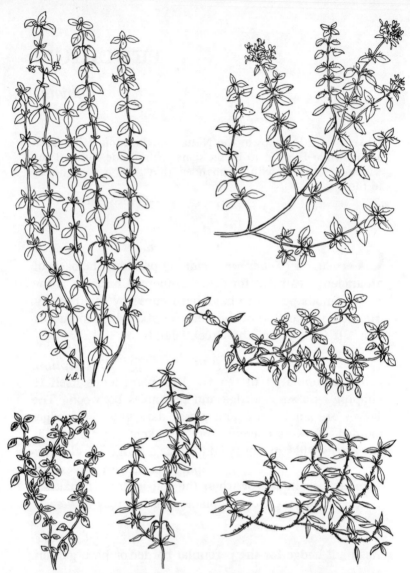

SIX EXCELLENT THYMES: (top left) lemon *Thymus Ser-pyllum vulgaris*, (top right) mother-of-thyme *T. Serpyllum*, (center right) 'Golden Lemon' *T. S. aureus*, (bottom left) 'Silver Lemon' *T. S. argenteus*, (bottom center) 'Narrowleaf French' *T. vulgaris*, (bottom right) woolly-stemmed *T. lanicaulis*

THYMUS

Labiatae

The Serpyllum Thyme

The *Serpyllum* group is divided into those thymes of flat or creeping growth (not over 3 in.) and those that form mats (to 6 in. while in flower, with well-established plants growing even taller). Some are gold-leaved, some misty blue-green or gray-green, others between dark green and chartreuse.

T. Serpyllum. The famous mother-of-thyme will grow and perpetuate itself under trying conditions. The dark and shiny leaves vary in size, but all give off the true thyme fragrance. Plants grow well among rocks and along terraces where they can work their way down a hill.

T. S. albus. This tiny, white-flowered plant is often overrun by more rampant types. It has the smallest bright-green leaves of all the thymes and is lemon-scented. In June lovely white blossoms appear.

T. S. argenteus. 'Silver Lemon' grows to 6 in. in shrub-like form. It is attractive in a solid bed or used as an accent. The green leaves are variegated with silver. 'Silver Lemon' needs a sheltered place where the temperature does not exceed 50 degrees or go below freezing, with evenly moist soil and ample fresh air on sunny winter days. A coldframe is a good place for winter storage of tender plants.

T. S. aureus. 'Golden Lemon' has green leaves edged with gold and a strong lemon odor. Blossoms come late. They are a light purple on a shrub about 6 in. high. The plant needs winter protection.

T. S. 'Caprilands.' Spice-scented, this is one of the best mat-forming thymes. The narrow leaves are light green, growing first as mats and later becoming thick cushions. Blooms appear in late July. Clip them back as they fade. It is a good plant to cover arid banks or terraces and even grows on the shaded side of a house.

T. S. 'Clear Gold' or 'Gold-leaved.' An excellent terrace cover, this yields a fine pungent odor when trod upon. At certain times of the year it turns a tarnished gold, but seedlings appearing around the parent plants in spring have bright, clear coloring. It grows well in dry seasons and in late July and August produces pale-lavender blooms that need to be cut back to avoid a ragged appearance. Tops die back in winter and need to be sheared off in spring to allow for new growth.

T. S. coccineus. The popular crimson thyme has small leaves set close. It stays dark green until autumn, when it turns red. Blossoms are a brilliant magenta-pink. The young seedlings flower late and extend the blooming time from June into July. *T. S. c. Splendens* is similar but has larger blooms.

T. S. conglomerata. A green-leaved thyme, it grows into a heavy mass. As the roots spread, each group of little branches forms a small circle. The plant is very hardy, surviving drought, flood, and cold.

T. S. lanuginosus. The woolly thyme is the lowest growing of the gray ones. It is also one of the most attractive of all the creepers, so gray it is hard to distinguish from the rock it covers. The gray wisps grow into woolly mats with a few pink flowers in late June. *T. S. l.* 'Hall's Woolly' has greener leaves than those of

116

T. S. lanuginosus, yet they are still gray, and the plants are much hardier and better as ground covers.

T. S. micans. A low, mound-forming thyme with small shiny leaves, it makes a compact carpet and bears purple flowers in June.

T. S. 'Misty Green.' Almost flat, this is excellent to trail over the edges of beds. It transplants easily to make a thick misty-green carpet with a certain grayness, as if it were covered by dew. Small pink blooms appear in August. Although 'Misty Green' is similar to *T. S. lanuginosus*, it is not so gray and is far more vigorous and compact, with no problem of winter killing.

T. S. nummularis. The marjoram-leaved thyme is a green plant with a gray cast. It makes a high, cushioned mat and blooms late in summer with purple flowers.

T. S. 'Nutmeg.' The dark-green leaves of the plant grow close to the ground and make a fast cover. When crushed, the leaves yield a spicy odor. The purple flowers appear in July and continue through August.

T. S. 'Pine-scented.' This has an unmistakable odor.

T. S. roseus. This is similar to *T. S. albus* in leaf and growth habit, but the leaf is more rounded and the flowers are rose-colored.

T. S. vulgaris (syn. *T. S. citriodorus*). The much-loved lemon thyme has dark-green shiny leaves. Taller than other varieties of *T. Serpyllum*, it has the same trait of rooting at the sides, and once established, increases rapidly. It winters well but does better if covered by an airy mulch of salt hay. Lemon thyme makes a good tea and provides fragrant green material for arrangements.

The Common Thymes

The common thymes (*T. vulgaris*) are used for seasoning and are traditionally a part of every culinary garden. They are, however, so fragrant and attractive that many gardeners now plant them as shrubby hedges to border paths and outline beds. These hedges are low—not over 12 in.—and may be trimmed for conformity. Clippings can be dried for seasonings and potpourri or for tea.

T. vulgaris 'Broadleaf English.' Similar to *T. Serpyllum* in leaf, it grows less shrubby than *T. v.* 'Narrowleaf French' and is especially good for cutting, as there is an abundance of leaf and stem. The little bushes thicken quickly, so that side roots can be pulled off for planting; they become established plants in a few weeks.

T. v. 'Narrowleaf English.' This is similar to 'Narrowleaf French,' but greener. Sow seeds in spring for plants that will mature the next year and be large enough for winter window boxes. Seedlings tolerate the change from garden to house better than older plants.

T. v. 'Narrowleaf French.' Older plants of this shrubby thyme are woody and gnarled like old trees. Young plants are stiff and straight; the color is definitely gray. The odor is sweeter than that of 'Broadleaf English.' It pays to protect this variety in winter with salt hay or pine boughs. It has small white blooms.

T. Zygis. This is a tiny shrub that grows to 4 in. It is similar to *T. vulgaris*, with slender leaves and white flowers. The variety *gracilis* sends up chartreuse branches from a creeping stem to 5 in. and has lance-shaped leaves with pale-pink flowers in July. These, along with *T. vulgaris*, provide much of the thymol of commerce.

Other Favorite Thymes

T. augustifolius. The green plant is given a gray appearance by a narrow, long leaf that is hairy. It is vigorous, spreads rapidly, and flowers in late June.

T. britannicus. This gray-leaved plant is excellent for covering large areas. The leaves, larger than those of *T. Serpyllum lanuginosus*, have the same formation and

118

are round, woolly, and sweet-scented. They are gray in dry weather, greener in rain, reddish or purple in spring and fall. Pink-lavender flowers appear in late June.

T. cimicinus. A vigorous and hardy import from southern Russia, this has reddish stems that creep along the ground, never reaching more than 3 in. *Cimicinus* means "smelling of bugs"; it smells like that when trod upon.

T. glaber (syn. *T. Chamaedrys*). Sometimes called Scandinavian thyme, this is a delightful plant. It makes a low glossy hedge to 3 in. The leaves, relatively large, are smooth and shiny and a deep blue-green. The reddish-purple blooms appear in July and August.

T. Herba-barona. This caraway-scented thyme from Corsica has long trailing stems and leaves. It is a fine ground cover, but it does not multiply rapidly.

T. lanicaulis. This woolly-stemmed thyme develops long arms to grasp whatever gets in the way. The pink blossoms are larger than those of most thymes, and bees delight in them. It is good for difficult spots.

T. Marschallianus. This low, mat-forming plant has long light-green leaves and a resinous odor. The flowers are pale lavender.

🕮 *Culture and Uses:* Thyme likes good drainage and filtered sun or full sun for only part of the day. Alkaline or sweet soil and rocks to clamber over are requisites. The seeds of *T. Serpyllum* germinate sparsely; those of *T. vulgaris* germinate freely, but the plants are slow to develop. The roots of plants must be well covered with soil, and newly planted beds must be protected from the sun. A winter mulch of salt hay or pine boughs is recommended.

Throughout history thyme has had innumerable medical uses. Today thyme is used for headaches, nerves, colds, and fevers. Thyme vinegar is used to ward off insects, to treat bites, and as a suntan lotion. Oil of thyme is used as a counterirritant for rheumatism and as an antiseptic for ringworm and burns.

119

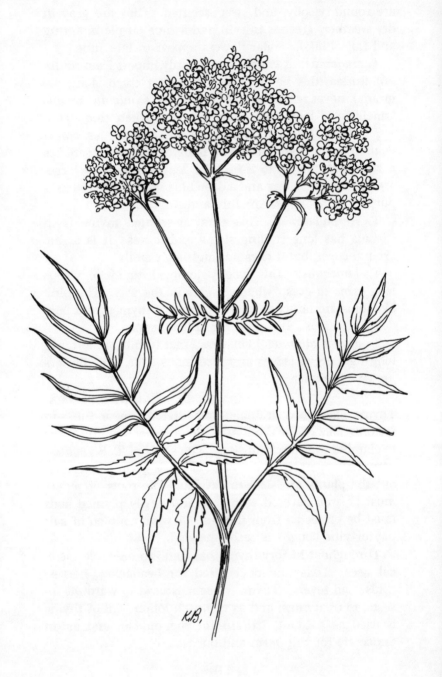

K.B.

VALERIANA

Valerianaceae

Then springen herbes grete and smale,
The licoris and the setewale.
—Chaucer

Garden heliotrope (*Valeriana officinalis*), also called phu, all-heal, setewale, and capon's tail, is a fragrant medicinal herb. While the carrion odor of the root is unpleasant to humans, it is relished by cats, dogs, and rats (it has been used as a ratbait). The root has been used as a drug to promote sleep, to quieten and soothe nerves, to cure insomnia, to treat epilepsy and in heart medicines for palpitations. Asiatic variations of *V. officinalis* were used as spices and perfumes.

ᕦ *Description:*
Hardy perennial, 3 to 5 ft. Leaves lance-shaped in pairs. Flowers pale pink in flattened cluster, or cyme, at intervals during the summer, starting in June. They are sweet, smelling of heliotrope.

ᕦ *Uses:*
As an attractive flowering herb for the back of the border.

ᕦ *Culture:*
Sun or shade in rich, moist garden soil. Propagate by removing sideshoots of old plants. Set firmly and deeply so that animals will not catch the odor of the root and dig it up.

121

K·B·

VIOLA

Violaceae

Reform the errours of the Spring;
Make that the tulips may have share
Of sweetness, seeing they are fair;
And Roses of their Thorns disarm:
   But most procure
That Violets may a longer Age endure.
          —Andrew Marvell

Violets (*Viola* species) of all types are important plants for the herb garden. The heart's-ease violas were used as a love-charm in Shakespeare's day, as a symbol of the Trinity in monastery gardens, as a medicine for eczema, and the flowers were cordials for the heart. The roots and seeds were used as purgatives.

Description:
V. odorata is the sweet English violet. *V. tricolor* is the heart's-ease or Johnny-jump-up, ever a favorite of poets and herbalists.

Uses:
Attractive border and ground cover. Candy the flowers for use on tops of cakes. Use them fresh in punch, in flower arrangements, and in miniature winter plantings where they will provide bloom out of season. Violets appeared in many food and drink recipes of the past, some of which have been revived. Violets appear in the May wine along with strawberries, and there is a violet jelly, a violet sherbet, and I have heard of violet fritters.

Culture:
Partial to full shade in humusy, moist soil. Propagate by dividing well-established clumps after they finish blooming. Guard violets closely or they will become troublesome weeds. *V. tricolor* or Johnny-jump-up is a self-sowing annual.

123

Index

Herbs are indexed by their common names if that name differs from the horticultural name.